I0048093

The New Workplace in Japan

SKILLS FOR A STRONG RECOVERY

OECD

BETTER POLICIES FOR BETTER LIVES

This work is published under the responsibility of the Secretary-General of the OECD. The opinions expressed and arguments employed herein do not necessarily reflect the official views of the Member countries of the OECD.

This document, as well as any data and map included herein, are without prejudice to the status of or sovereignty over any territory, to the delimitation of international frontiers and boundaries and to the name of any territory, city or area.

Please cite this publication as:
OECD (2022), *The New Workplace in Japan: Skills for a Strong Recovery*, Getting Skills Right, OECD Publishing, Paris, https://doi.org/10.1787/7c897f52-en.

ISBN 978-92-64-86888-5 (print)
ISBN 978-92-64-40075-7 (pdf)
ISBN 978-92-64-69226-8 (HTML)
ISBN 978-92-64-76867-3 (epub)

Getting Skills Right
ISSN 2520-6117 (print)
ISSN 2520-6125 (online)

Foreword

The COVID-19 pandemic sparked one of the sharpest contractions in economic activity in living memory. A swifter than expected recovery followed, but the crisis exposed a number of flaws in the current labour market and skills systems in many, if not all, countries. The extent to which workers can adapt to changes in the type and content of jobs depends critically on the readiness and flexibility of adult learning systems to help people develop and maintain relevant skills over their working careers.

Digitalisation of key public services, such as employment support, career guidance and training, as well as adoption of teleworking practices, have altered the way in which adults navigate the labour market and have the potential to help address challenges brought about by economic disruptions and rapidly changing skills needs. Such services are particularly important in the aftermath of the COVID-19 pandemic, as many adults are faced with new ways of working and learning.

This report reviews Japan's employment policy response during and immediately after the COVID-19 pandemic, and provides policy recommendations to improve the responsiveness of the adult learning system to changing skills needs, by strengthening training provision, broadening access to career guidance and fostering teleworking. Chapter 1 reviews recent labour market developments in Japan, and discusses how the skill composition of the Japanese workforce changed during the pandemic. Chapter 2 discusses employment policy responses to the pandemic, including employment and training subsidies, teleworking and career guidance. Chapter 3 focuses on persistent inequalities in skills and training, and offers suggestions on how Japan can create more responsive training policies through the use of well-integrated labour market information systems.

This report was prepared by Michele Tuccio, Nozomi Ohno and Dzana Topalovic from the Skills and Employability Division of the Directorate for Employment Labour and Social Affairs (ELS). The work was carried out under the supervision of Glenda Quintini (Manager of the Skills Team) and Mark Keese (Head of the Skills and Employability Division). The report benefitted also from the useful feedback of Mark Pearson (Deputy Director of ELS). The OECD Secretariat would like to thank the Japanese Ministry of Health, Labour and Welfare, the Japan Institute for Labour Policy and Training, and the Panel Data Research Center at Keio University for their support in carrying out this project.

This report is published under the responsibility of the Secretary General of the OECD, with the financial assistance of the Japanese Ministry of Health, Labour and Welfare. The views expressed in this report should not be taken to reflect the official position of OECD member countries.

Table of contents

FIGURES

TABLES

Follow OECD Publications on:

https://twitter.com/OECD

https://www.facebook.com/theOECD

https://www.linkedin.com/company/organisation-eco-cooperation-development-organisation-cooperation-developpement-eco/

https://www.youtube.com/user/OECDiLibrary

https://www.oecd.org/newsletters/

Abbreviations and acronyms

Cedefop	European Centre for the Development of Vocational Training
EACEA	European Education and Culture Executive Agency
EOPPEP	National Organization for Certification of Qualifications & Vocational Guidance
ETF	European Training Foundation
JILPT	Japan Institute for Labour Policy and Training
JPY	Japanese Yen
JPSED	Japanese Panel Study of Employment Dynamics
ICT	Information and communication technology
ILO	International Labour Organization
LMIS	Labour market information system
METI	Japanese Ministry of Economy, Trade and Industry
MIC	Japanese Ministry of Internal Affairs and Communications
MHLW	Japanese Ministry of Health, Labour and Welfare
OECD	Organisation for Economic Co-operation and Development
PES	Public Employment Services
PIAAC	OECD's Programme for the International Assessment of Adult Competencies (Survey of Adult Skills)
SCGA	OECD 2020 Survey of Career Guidance for Adults
SMEs	Small and medium-sized enterprises
UNESCO	United Nations Educational, Scientific and Cultural Organization

Executive summary

At a time when the global COVID-19 pandemic has profoundly altered the type and content of jobs, investing in skills is more important than ever to build resilient and inclusive labour markets. Ongoing policy efforts to make the Japanese labour market more inclusive were disrupted by the pandemic as the government's focus quickly shifted to dealing with the state of emergency and countering the negative consequences of a global lockdown. The policy responses have been largely successful, with the Japanese labour market experiencing limited increases in unemployment compared to other OECD countries. Yet, the pandemic has altered the labour market in ways that are only starting to become evident and that will provide new challenges for policy makers in the years to come. Now, more than ever, Japan's policy makers must strengthen the adult learning system to make individuals and enterprises more responsive to change and foster stronger growth and well-being.

Initial policy responses to the pandemic-induced disruptions were swift and efficient. Existing employment support measures were expanded and new ones introduced, which avoided mass dismissals. Unemployment rose only slightly to 3.1% (seasonally adjusted) in October 2020, and has since decreased, though by June 2022 it had not yet returned to its pre-pandemic level of 2.2% in December 2019. However, employees were affected in other ways, such as by a reduction in earnings and working hours. The adoption of teleworking practices and the digitalisation of key services such as employment support, career guidance and training also helped keep unemployment low. While Japan still lags behind other OECD countries in implementing these practices, the pandemic provided a momentum that should be leveraged to foster more flexible adult learning provision and address many of the barriers that adults face when upskilling and reskilling, such as time constraints and lack of easy access to information.

Women, non-regular workers and low-skilled workers, whose labour market outcomes were already below average, bore the brunt of the pandemic negative effects, experiencing more unemployment and inactivity than other socio-economic groups. Further, those who worked in companies focusing more on hours worked over delivery of final outputs were less likely to teleworking.

In addition to its impact on employment and unemployment, the pandemic has changed the demand for skills in Japan. An innovative analysis using individual-level data shows that social and analytical skills have become more prominent in the Japanese labour market in the initial post-pandemic period, compared with previous years. Further, the pre-pandemic increase in the importance of manual skills seems to be inverting, suggesting that social-distancing and digitalisation may be raising the demand for interpersonal and problem-solving skills while reducing manual handling. The analysis, which also features an overview of skill composition in Japan, shows that women are less likely than men to be employed in positions that require leadership or technical skills, while non-regular employees are more concentrated in occupations making lower use of most skills than regular workers. The new data underlying the analysis has the potential to provide valuable evidence for policy makers to develop effective upskilling and reskilling programmes and make the labour market more resilient.

Key recommendations

To foster the development of the skills needed for a strong recovery, the OECD recommends that Japan:

Take stock of the lessons learnt during the pandemic:

- Improve the monitoring of employment adjustment subsidies to gather better take-up data.
- Assess the effectiveness of job retention schemes in protecting different types of workers from the risk of unemployment and in supporting longer-term career paths.
- Continue to promote the digitalisation of administrative services.
- Provide basic digital skills programmes to promote a broader take-up of online career guidance, online learning and teleworking opportunities.

Support the digitalisation of career guidance services:

- Promote career guidance services through more online provision.
- Accompany online career guidance with in-person counselling in order to provide comprehensive support to those most removed from the labour market.

Foster the adoption of teleworking practices:

- Strengthen support for the introduction of teleworking particularly for small and medium-sized enterprises.
- Support the expansion of more diverse work styles.
- Collect and disseminate good practice examples about teleworking, including on how to improve communication among employees and how to ensure effective labour management.
- Improve work flexibility by further expanding the flextime system (flexible working arrangement) while paying attention to ensuring workers' health and actively introduce ICT equipment in public workplaces.

Support the expansion of online training:

- Support both private and public providers who want to implement distance learning, through technical assistance and certification of full online training for public providers.
- Consider additional subsidies for training providers who want to trial delivery of real-time online learning and on-demand recorded training courses.

Support the scaling up of modular provision and micro-credentials in training:

- Introduce skills profiling and personalised learning pathways to tailor adults learning courses to their skills and experience.
- Promote and recognise training programmes where shorter modules are rewarded with partial credits, and can be stacked to attain a fully-credited training programme that is recognised by the government.

Increase training participation of groups with lower labour market outcomes:

- Exploit skills composition analysis to understand the best upskilling and reskilling opportunities for women and non-regular workers to ensure they are not 'left behind' in the post-pandemic recovery.

- Leverage career guidance and upskilling opportunities to increase hiring of women in positions where they are underrepresented.

Leverage existing data to assess and anticipate skills needs:

- Perform an extensive mapping of existing data sources on employment and skills and key indicators that can be tracked to analyse changes in skills supply and demand. Create an overview of the data.

- Set up a labour market information system (LMIS), potentially exploiting real-time big-data, and involve all key stakeholders. Evaluate which public institution or department is best equipped to manage the programme.

- Create a structured dissemination plan for the LMIS to feed into employment, training and migration programmes.

1 How the labour market and skills needs in Japan are changing during the COVID-19 crisis

In general, the Japanese labour market has avoided many of the negative consequences of the COVID-19 crisis observed internationally; a small number of industries and some socio-economic groups have borne the brunt of the pandemic's effect. This chapter first provides an overview of the impact of the pandemic on the labour market, focusing particularly on those segments of the workforce most affected. It then discusses how the demand and supply of skills had been changing prior to the pandemic. Finally, using innovative methods, the chapter presents an overview of skill requirements in the Japanese labour market and how the pandemic has affected key skills trends.

In Brief

The pandemic has accelerated pre-existing skills trends in Japan

The COVID-19 crisis has put pressure on the Japanese labour market and amplified existing challenges. Though government interventions have kept the unemployment rate relatively stable, the employment of women and non-regular workers has taken a hit. Industries such as restaurants and accommodation have experienced large fluctuations in both employment and earnings. In order to offset declining economic activity, caused by confinement and social distancing, many companies and workers reduced earnings and working hours.

Japanese adults face a challenging labour market situation after the pandemic, and pre-existing skills imbalances are putting into question whether the Japanese labour force has the appropriate skills required in the post-COVID-19 economy. Innovative analysis that map the occupational structure of the Japanese economy to the corresponding skill requirements show that foundational and social skills are the most commonly required skills in existing jobs while relatively few workers are in jobs requiring advanced cognitive skills and mathematics and programming. Only moderate technical skills are in high demand in Japan, driven by the larger share of craft and trade occupations relative to advanced engineering. At the same time, the demand for social and analytical skills has increased, especially during the pandemic.

1.1. The COVID-19 crisis and recovery in Japan

The COVID-19 pandemic had mixed effects on the Japanese economy, setting in motion changes in business activities and affecting people's lives. After the confirmation of Japan's first case of coronavirus on 15 January 2020, the government requested the cancellation, postponement, or scaling down of social events attracting a large number of people, as well as the temporary closure of elementary and junior high schools from March through the Spring Break. However, the number of infected people continued to increase, and the first wave reached its peak of 644 positive cases per day in April 2020. In order to limit the spread of the virus, the Japanese Government declared a state of emergency in seven prefectures, including the Tokyo metropolitan area, requesting residents to refrain from going out and companies to close their businesses temporarily.

In spite of Japan's relatively low infection rates compared to other OECD countries like Italy or the United Kingdom, the government adopted a number of large-scale emergency economic measures, totalling as high as JPY 120 trillion, as an initial response to the COVID-19 outbreak (Cabinet Office, 2020[1]). Measures during this initial phase focused in particular on safeguarding employment and businesses by greatly expanding job retention schemes and by strengthening the counselling and support system for jobseekers. In addition, Japan was one of very few OECD countries offering a flat-rate cash payment of JPY 100 000 to all its residents to help people make ends meet (OECD, 2020[2]) (a careful analysis the policy response of the Japanese Government during the pandemic will be presented in Chapter 2). As a result of the first wave of COVID-19 contagions, Japan's real GDP recorded a significant decline in the second quarter of 2020: -7.9% compared to the previous quarter.

The late spring in 2020 brought a moment of relief in the fight against the pandemic in Japan, with the number of infected people shrinking from 12 089 in April to 1 747 in June. Encouraged by the positive health outcomes, the government actively promoted a few economic stimulus measures, such as the "Go to Travel" subsidy programme aimed at boosting the demand for domestic tourism. Yet, the number of infected people gradually surged again during the end of the summer and the fall of 2020, reaching as high as 154 700 in January 2021 and leading to the declaration of a new state of emergency. The Japanese Government responded to the negative impacts of the second wave of infections with the approval of a new set of economic measures. In addition to the maintenance of job retentions schemes, the new policies were also characterised by an expansion of the public support to cover the promotion of labour mobility, including support for changing jobs and industries.

After the first year of the health crisis, the consequences for the Japanese economy were multiple. Output dropped as sanitary restrictions restrained consumption and investment. Real GDP declined by 4.5% in 2020 from the previous year while the reduced economic activity reflected in a 5.2% decrease in private consumption. The global economic slowdown and momentary disruption of supply chains led to a 6.9% decrease in imports and an 11.7% decrease in exports. Exports have since rebounded as major trading partners have recovered and are set to remain firm, while other indicators showed a sluggish recovery in 2021. Similarly, due to the restrictions put in place by the government on people entering the country from overseas, the number of foreign visitors to Japan in 2020 was only 4.12 million, a huge decrease of 87% from the previous year (Ministry of Land, Infrastructure, Transport and Tourism, 2021[3]).

Vaccinations against the coronavirus for health care workers started in February 2021, expanding to the elderly in April. In the meantime, the government announced a new employment and training package aimed at strengthening vocational training (e.g. by opening public vocational training courses that could be completed in a shorter period of time than in the past, and setting up more online training courses). Further, the government decided to provide an additional cash payment of JPY 50 000 per child in March 2021 as a livelihood support for low-income child-rearing households.

The total number of infected people reached again a record high (567 572) in August 2021. Only in October 2021 did the Japanese Government decide to lift the third state of emergency, which had been in effect since April. Subsequent waves of infection have resulted in higher numbers of positive cases (peaking at almost 100 000 cases per day in February 2022), but containment measures have been less strict than in the initial phases of the pandemic.

Over the past two years of the health crisis, the entire Japanese labour market has been shaken by the COVID-19 pandemic. Health concerns and restrictions on mobility strongly affected the way both employers and employees conducted their work activities. All of a sudden and with a quick turnaround, companies had to review their work styles and be innovative in order to continue operating. Teleworking became one of the main solutions to prevent businesses from closing, in addition to reduction in face-to-face interactions through staggered work schedules and bicycle commuting. As a result of the changes in companies' behaviour, some workers saw a decrease in their working hours and earnings. At the same time companies were able to keep much of their staff employed thanks to government-led retention schemes, and the government's digital shift allowed for online career guidance and online learning programmes to be implemented. However, there is still little use of labour market information systems to help align the supply and demand of skills in the labour market. To shed new light on the profound changes brought on by the COVID-19 pandemic, the remainder of this report presents in details how Japan's labour market and skills needs have transformed and are still evolving in the recovery from the crisis.

Figure 1.1. The evolution of the COVID-19 crisis in Japan

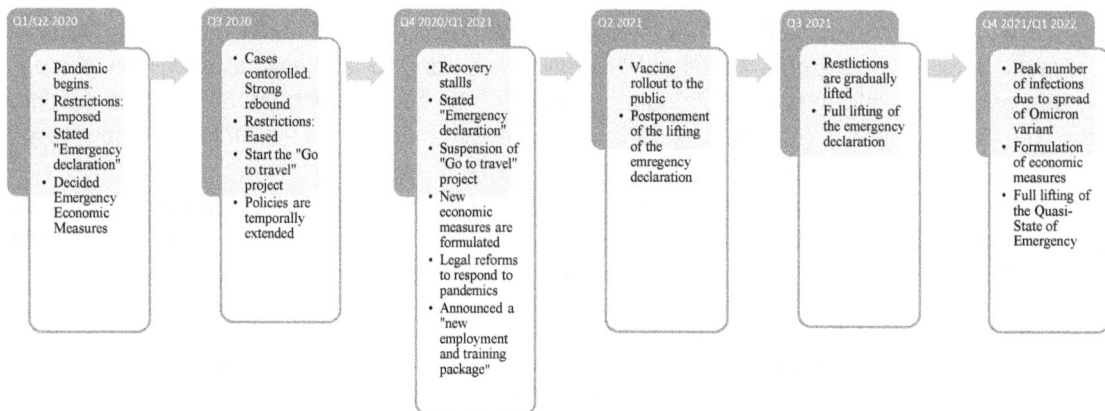

Q1/Q2 2020	Q3 2020	Q4 2020/Q1 2021	Q2 2021	Q3 2021	Q4 2021/Q1 2022
• Pandemic begins. • Restrictions: Imposed • Stated "Emergency declaration" • Decided Emergency Economic Measures	• Cases contorolled. Strong rebound • Restrictions: Eased • Start the "Go to travel" project • Policies are temporally extended	• Recovery stallls • Stated "Emergency declaration" • Suspension of "Go to travel" project • New economic measures are formulated • Legal reforms to respond to pandemics • Announced a "new employment and training package"	• Vaccine rollout to the public • Postponement of the lifting of the emrergency declaration	• Restlictions are gradually lifted • Full lifting of the emergency declaration	• Peak number of infections due to spread of Omicron variant • Formulation of economic measures • Full lifting of the Quasi-State of Emergency

Source: Authors' elaboration.

1.2. The impact of the crisis on the Japanese labour market

1.2.1. Overall employment rates decreased only marginally in Japan during the COVID-19 pandemic

Around the world, the COVID-19 pandemic led to an unprecedented economic and employment crisis. Efforts to contain the spread of the virus led to numerous countries closing their borders and severe contractions in many economic activities. In the majority of OECD countries, lockdowns and uncertainty about the national and global outlook resulted in fall in employment rates and a surge in unemployment and inactivity. In the OECD, the employment rate started declining in February 2020, with the quarterly employment rate falling from 68.9% in Q4 2019 to 63.5% in Q2 2020 for people aged 15-64 (seasonally adjusted) (OECD, 2021[4]). In a few countries, the decline has been even steeper. For instance, employment fell by 11 percentage points between January 2020 and April 2020 in both Canada and the United States (Figure 1.2).[1]

By contrast, in Japan the COVID-19 pandemic led to only a minor decrease in the employment rate. In fact, although the pandemic reached Japan relatively early, its effects have been less drastic than in other OECD countries. Japan's employment rate dipped in May 2020 to 77% (0.8 percentage points less than in January 2020), and has since recovered to its pre-COVID-19 level. Successive waves of infection have had minor effects on the employment rate, but restrictions have led to more drastic declines in economic growth (OECD, 2021[5]).

The unemployment rate (seasonally adjusted) rose to 3.1% in October 2020 compared with the 2019 average of 2.4%, and has since declined to 2.6% in June 2022. Even though the unemployment rate has returned close to its pre-pandemic levels, the pace of recovery has been lacking in force, and total hours worked in the economy were still around 7% lower in June 2022 than in December 2019.

Figure 1.2. The overall employment rate has been affected only marginally in Japan

Monthly employment rate (aged 15-64)

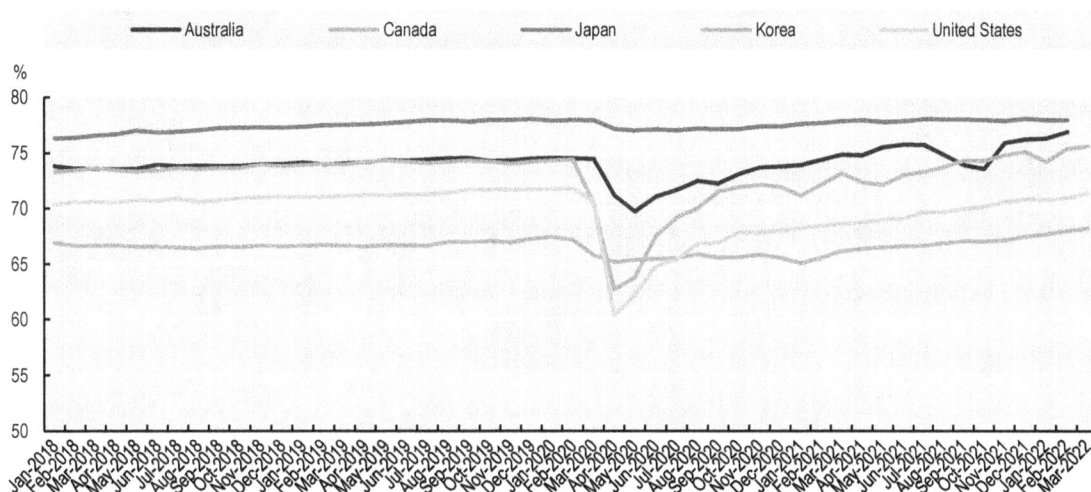

Source: OECD Short-Term Labour Market Statistics.

1.2.2. Women and young people were hit harder by the pandemic, deepening existing labour market divides

Though the pandemic did not cause a major fall in the overall employment rate, it did have a substantial impact on certain groups in Japan. Women and young people have borne the brunt of COVID-19 on the labour market, with young women aged 15-24 being most negatively affected (Figure 1.3). May 2020 saw the largest drop in the employment rate for young women aged 15-24 compared to May 2019 (-2.8 percentage points), and this negative trend continued over the year. Young men aged 15-24 are the second most affected group, with their largest drop being a -2.2 percentage points in the employment rate in October 2020 compared to October 2019. Women aged 25-54 have also been disproportionately affected by the pandemic when compared with their male counterparts.

The negative effect on women and young people reflects these groups being overrepresented in non-regular and part-time work (Yamaguchi, 2019[6]), as well as being more concentrated in service-oriented occupations, which were severely impacted by the crisis. Similar trends are evident in other OECD countries, where women and young adults accounted for the bulk of the labour force in affected industries (OECD, 2021[7]). The only demographic group recording a positive growth in the employment rate has been women aged 55-64. This is possibly due to the increase of women aged 55-59 in health care employment, especially due to the rising labour demand in the health and welfare industry. Data from the Japanese labour force survey shows that between June 2019 and 2020, employment rose by 80 000 people among women aged 55-59. Of that increase three out of four women age 55-59 year-old were employed in the health care sector.

Figure 1.3. Women and youth were impacted more than others

Percentage point change in monthly employment rate (aged 15-64), 2020 compared to 2019

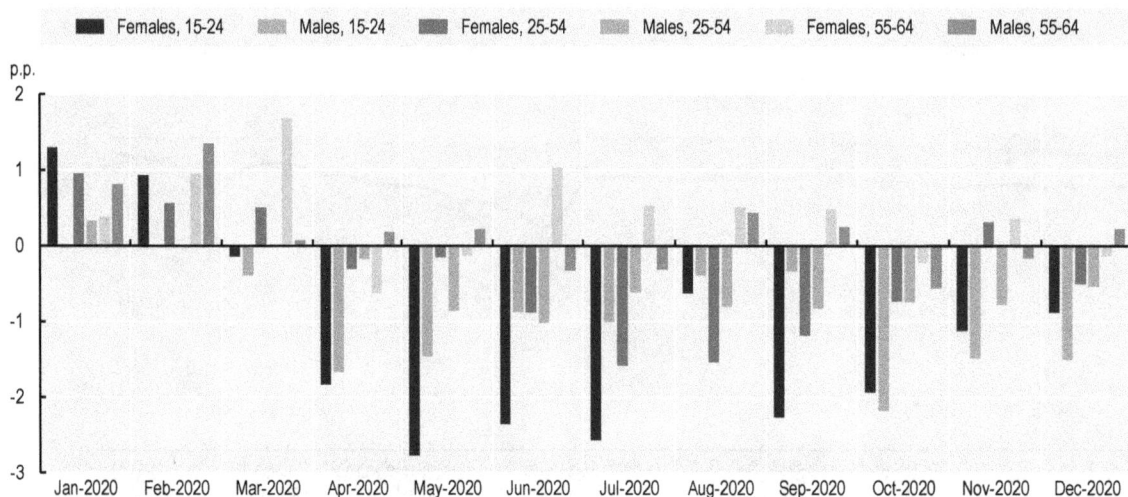

Note: p.p.: percentage points. Ratio to the same period of the preceding year.
Source: OECD Short-Term Labour Market Statistics.

Non-regular employment decreased more than regular employment, reflecting, on the one hand, the wide use of non-regular contracts in the exposed industries (such as in restaurants and hotels) and, on the other hand, the more unstable nature of non-regular job contracts. The number of people in regular employment has been on the rise for several years, and remained relatively stable during the pandemic and even displayed a slight increase, particularly for women. By contrast, non-regular employment suffered under the pressure of COVID-19, and in October 2021 there were nearly 1 million (920 000) fewer non-regular workers in the economy than in January 2020.

There is an unequal distribution of non-regular employment across genders. In January 2020, women made up a 68.5% of non-regular employees. In April 2020, there were 740 000 fewer women employed as non-regular workers compared with January 2019 (Figure 1.4). The proportion of women employed as regular workers has slightly increased since the start of the pandemic, yet total employment of women remained lower in 2021 than in 2019. In January 2022 there were 800 000 fewer women working in non-regular jobs than in January 2019. There were only minor fluctuation in the number of men employed during the crisis. Japan's tax and social security system is part of the explanation of why so many Japanese women work as non-regular employees. Indeed, women who make less than a designated ceiling are exempt from income tax and can be claimed by their husbands as dependent spouses, resulting in a substantial tax deduction for their household. Working full-time would not only lead to higher taxes, but the women would also be required to pay for their own health insurance and pension premiums. Although the government has in recent years undertaken tax reform and other measures to make tax and social security systems more favourable to second-earners, still many women opt for non-regular and part-time work (OECD, 2015[8]; Shibata, 2017[9]). However, non-regular status typically means lower pay, less generous benefits and higher job insecurity, especially during economic contractions.

Figure 1.4. Women in non-regular employment experienced the largest decrease during the pandemic

Number of employed as regular and non-regular employees, by gender, using January 2019 as base

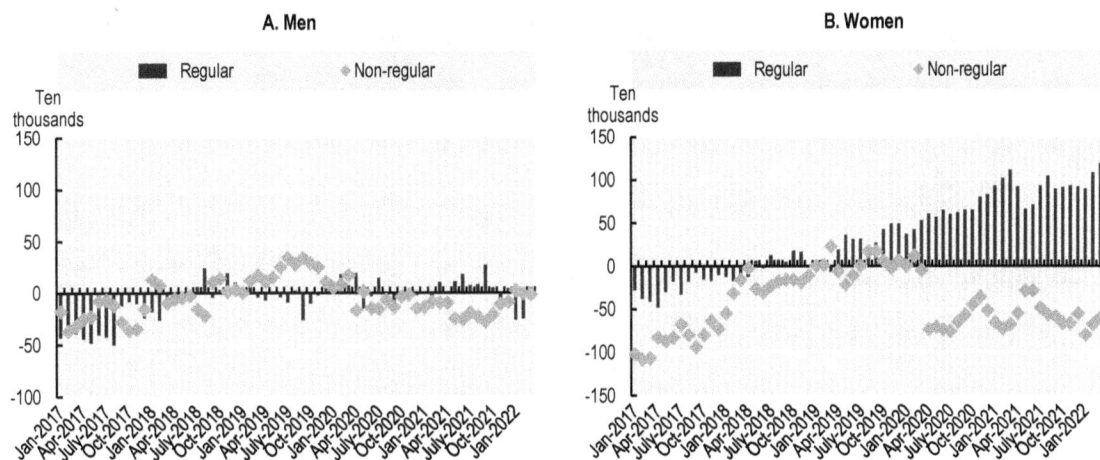

Note: Seasonally adjusted.
Source: Japanese Labour Force Survey.

Sectors and industries were affected differently by the need for social distancing, the temporary drop in consumer demand, and disruptions in global markets and supply chains due to the pandemic. Services that rely on face-to-face interactions, sales of non-essential goods and international movement experienced a large direct impact of containment and mitigation measures. Indeed, accommodation, food and personal services experienced the largest reduction in output and employment, with the greatest drop in 2020 in employment occurring in May (-0.90 percentage points compared to May 2019) (Figure 1.5). Agriculture and manufacturing all saw a decline in employment, though less drastic. These industries continued to experience decreasing levels of employment throughout 2020 and 2021 (with a couple of exceptions). The only sector that saw a continuous increase in the employment throughout the pandemic is the "other services" sector, likely due to the rise in demand of certain services such as health care, IT and other support services necessary during the pandemic.

Figure 1.5. Employment decreased in accommodation, food, and personal services, while it constantly increased in the other services sector even during the pandemic

Percentage point change in employment (aged 15+), year on year

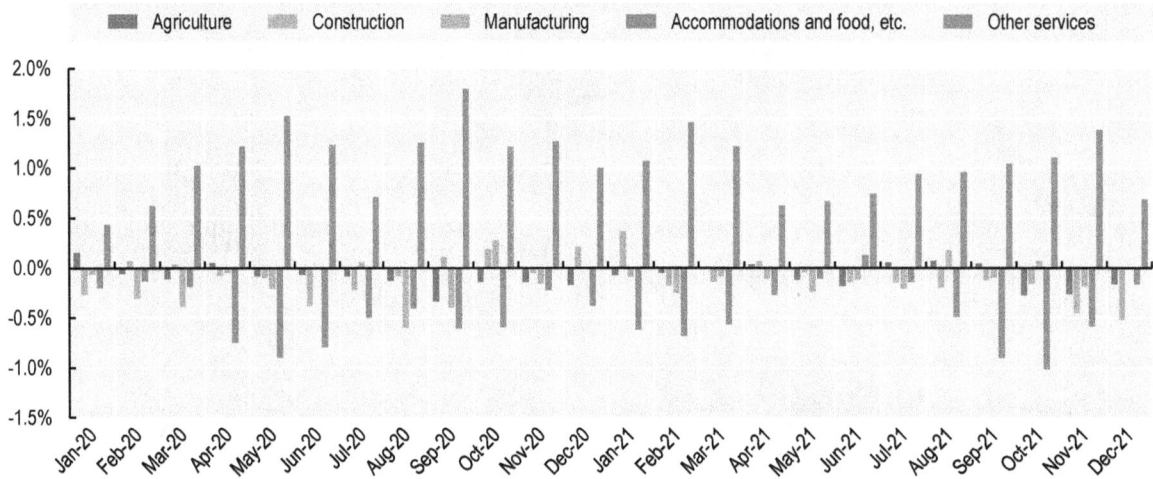

Note: Ratio to the same period of the preceding year. The industry of Accommodations and food, etc. refers to accommodations, eating and drinking services, living-related and personal services and amusement services.
Source: Japanese Labour Force Survey.

1.2.3. The pandemic had negative labour market impacts on inactivity and labour market participation, especially for women

The modest rise in unemployment in Japan during the crisis masks deeper impacts in the labour market. For instance, there was a sharp increase in inactivity among the working-age population in April 2020, where approximately 590 000 more people left the labour force compared to April 2019 (Figure 1.6). Inactivity continued to rise until November 2020. Unemployment peaked in December 2020 with 550 000 more people being unemployed compared to the same month in the preceding year.

The increase in inactivity was more prevalent among women, where 480 000 left the labour force in April 2020 compared with the previous year (by contrast, only 120 000 men became inactive during the same period). This is likely due to traditional gender roles linked to childcare and the closures of schools and childcare facilities. At the same time, women make up a larger share of non-regular workers, who are more likely to drop out of the labour force than regular workers. In contrast, men experienced more unemployment which peaked in November 2020 for this group, likely due to their concentration in affected industries such as construction and manufacturing and the prevalence of young adults in non-regular employment contracts.

Figure 1.6. The immediate response to the COVID-19 pandemic was a move from employment to inactivity, especially for many women

Change in working age population (aged 15+), 2020 compared to 2019, seasonally adjusted

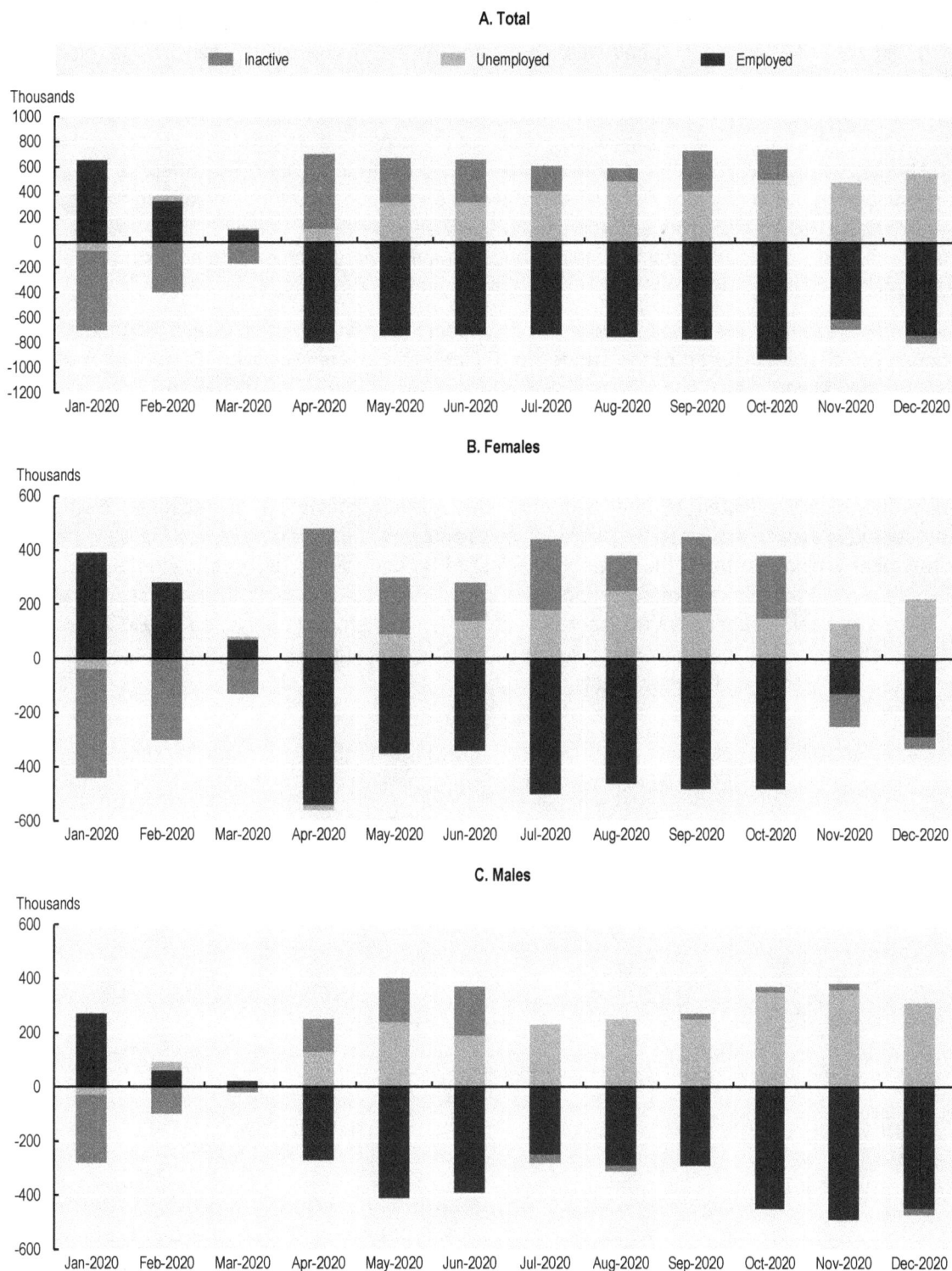

Source: OECD Short-Term Labour Market Statistics.

The gender employment gap has been declining for a number of years; however, the COVID-19 pandemic pushed the gap back to the same levels as the beginning of 2019 (Figure 1.7). The pandemic saw a rise in the gender employment gap from 13 percentage points in January 2019 to 14 percentage points in July 2020. Prior to the pandemic, the Japanese Government had implemented several policies to improve working conditions for women and increase women's labour force participation, but the projected effects of these policies were distorted due to the closure of day care centres and increase of women with home schooling responsibilities during the pandemic. As restrictions are easing and the economy is returning to normal, policies limiting working hours and increasing the provision of childcare places are having pronounced effects on the participation of mothers with young children, though demand for childcare still remains unmet. Yet, deregulation, unfavourable work contracts and low wages for day-care worker have led to a shortage of staff in day-care, in some cases forcing centres to close. The effective job-opening ratio (an indicator of how many jobs are available out of the total number of job seekers registered at the public employment service) for childcare workers in 2021 was more than twice as high as the average for all occupations, and the labour shortage remains serious, leaving many women with no options to alleviate the responsibilities of childcare (Ministry of Health, Labour and Welfare, 2022[10]).

Employers are becoming more accountable for increasing the labour participation of women. New legislation in effect since the start of the pandemic requires employers with over 100 regular workers to establish gender action plans and disclose related information (OECD, 2021[5]). As companies are committing to increase the hiring of women and improve their working conditions, it is likely that such policies have mitigated some of the negative employment effects of COVID-19 on women, but they have not been enough to offset the substantial unemployment and dropout rate of women in Japan. Women were disproportionally affected by the pandemic due to a combination of reasons. Women are overrepresented in service industries that were forced to shut down, they are more likely to be in part-time and non-regular employment and thus among the first to be considered for retrenchments, and during school lockdown women took on more caring roles in the household, leading to a reduction in working hours. There has been a substantial re-absorption of women into employment since July 2020, however this has largely been due to a pick-up in hiring of non-regular workers, who experience less stable employment, lower wages and fewer benefits.

Figure 1.7. After constant declines over the years, during the pandemic the gender employment rate gap in Japan returned to the same levels of the beginning of 2019

Gender employment rate gap, seasonally adjusted

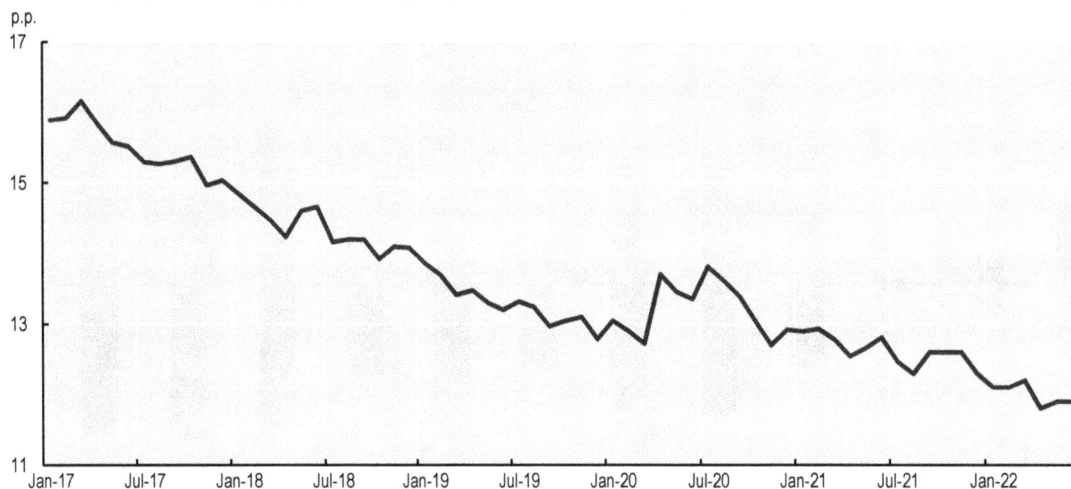

Note: p.p.: percentage points. The gap is calculated as the difference in employment rates between men and women aged 15-64 years old.
Source: OECD Short-Term Labour Market Statistics.

1.2.4. In order to absorb some of the labour market shocks of the pandemic, earnings and hours worked were drastically reduced

In addition to a rise in inactivity following the outbreak of the COVID-19 pandemic, the Japanese labour market also adjusted to the crisis through a substantial decrease in average earnings. Year-on-year changes in real earnings were already negative in 2019 but even larger falls occurred during the pandemic (Figure 1.8). The largest fall occurred in May 2020 with a 2.3 percentage point reduction compared with May 2019. Out of the G7 countries for which data is available, Japan saw the largest drop in hourly earnings in manufacturing during the crisis (Figure 1.9).

The reduction in real earnings is in part due to the decrease in base pay, but can mainly be attributed to a reduction in special pay (such as mid-year and end-year bonuses) and overtime pay (Leussink, 2021[11]). In fact, an analysis regarding changes in earnings before (2015-19) and after (2020) the outbreak of COVID-19, controlling for firm size, industry, employment type, and gender, shows that the monthly earnings level of women and non-regular workers fell significantly in 2020 compared to men and regular workers respectively, while the gap has narrowed compared to the pre-COVID-19 level when converted to hourly wages (Annex 1.A). By comparison, countries like the United States and Italy saw minimal disruptions to earnings in manufacturing, while the United Kingdom and Canada had large drops in earnings which quickly stabilised in the third quarter of 2020.

Figure 1.8. Real earnings declined in 2019 but steeper falls occurred during the pandemic

Percentage point change in real wages, year on year

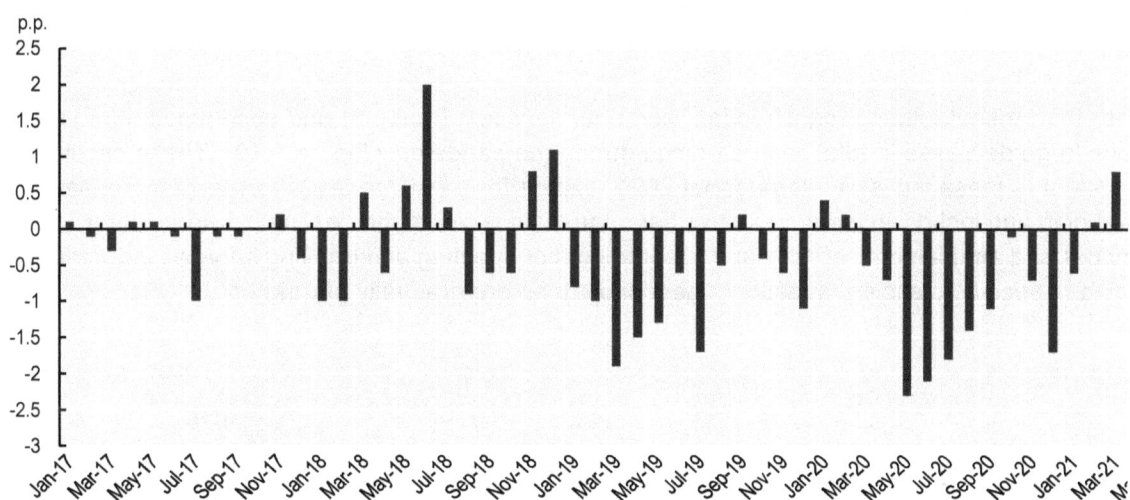

Note: p.p.: percentage points. Change in real earnings relative to the same period of the preceding year.
Source: Ministry of Health, Labour and Welfare, Monthly Labour Survey.

Figure 1.9. Out of the G7 countries for which data are available, Japan saw the largest drop in hourly earnings in manufacturing during the crisis

Hourly earnings index for manufacturing (2015=100), seasonally adjusted

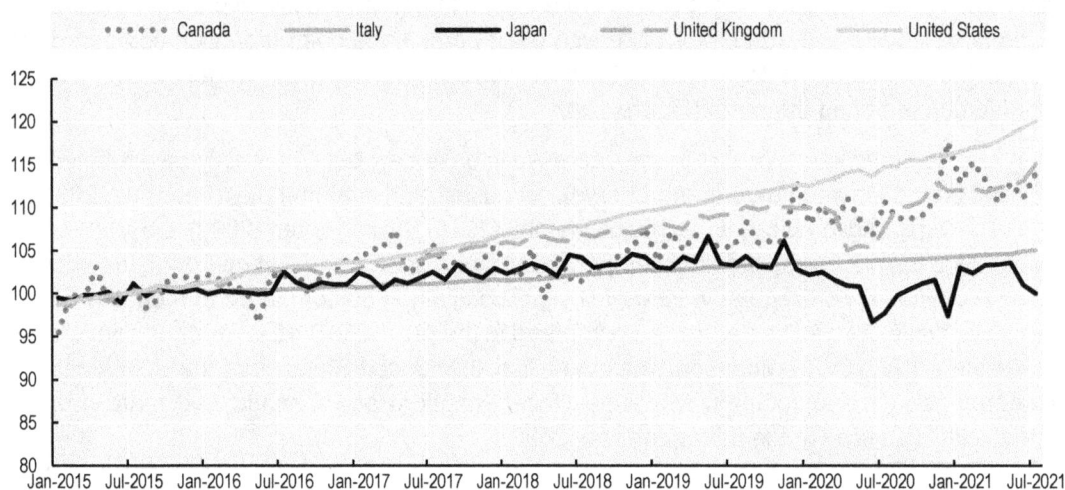

Note: Data refer to cash earnings of employees in the manufacturing industries before deductions for income taxes, social insurance contributions, union dues, payments for goods purchased, etc. Total cash earnings include contractual cash earnings (scheduled cash earnings and overtime pay) plus special cash earnings (retroactive payments of wages, payments such as summer and year-end bonuses, marriage allowances). Data for Japan refer to manufacturing as defined in the Japan Standard Industrial Classification, and cover establishments with 30 or more employees selected from the latest Establishment Census.
Source: OECD Main Economic Indicators (MEI).

Other than manufacturing, construction, personal services, transport and accommodation industries saw a large decrease in total cash earnings during the pandemic (Figure 1.10). These declines were persistent in these industries throughout 2021, except for a few modest short-term increases. Social distancing and lockdown measures have been the main driver of the decline in living-related, personal services and amusement services and accommodations, eating and drinking services industries Since easing of social distancing measures, these industries are gradually picking up.

Figure 1.10. Construction, personal services, transport and accommodation industries saw the largest decrease in earnings during the pandemic

Percentage point change in total cash earnings, year on year

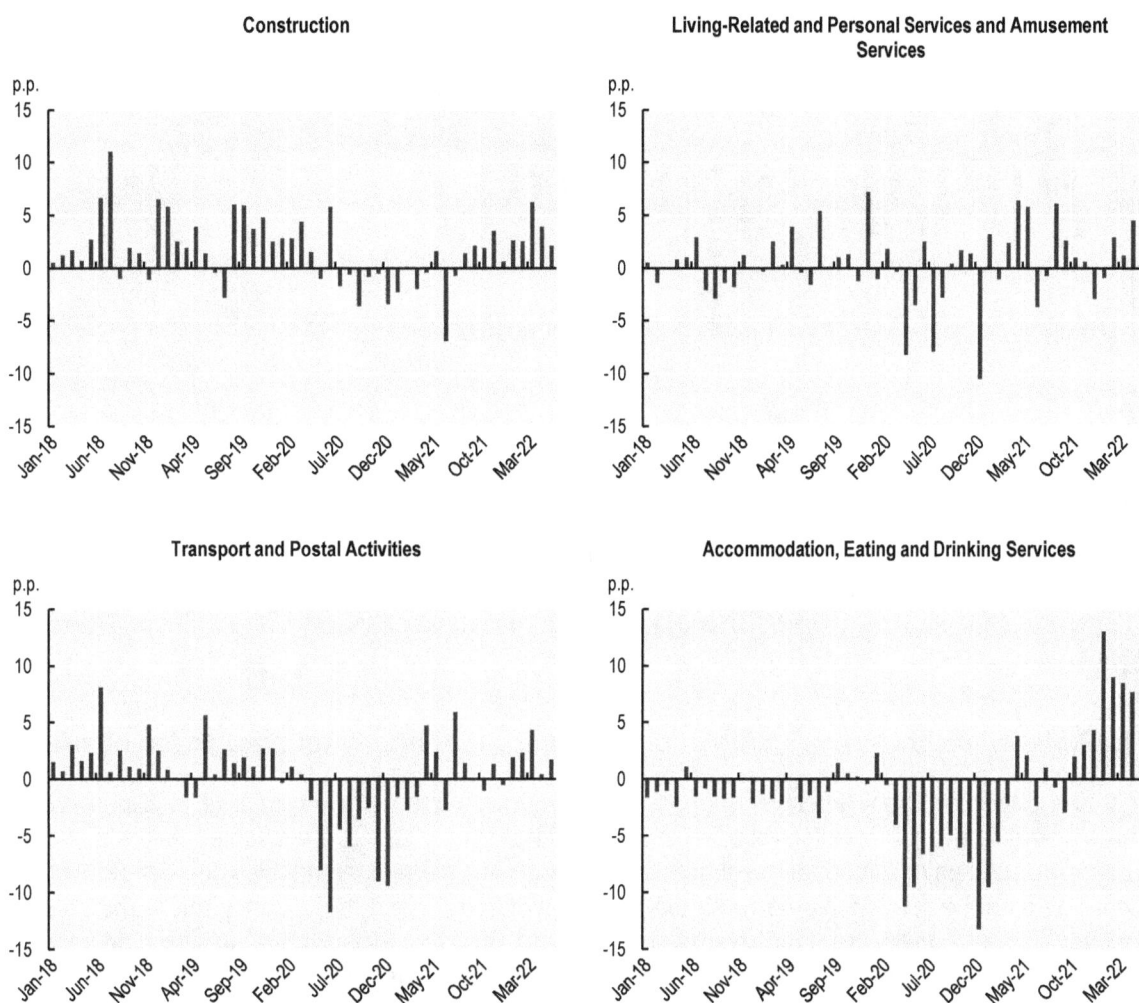

Construction

Living-Related and Personal Services and Amusement Services

Transport and Postal Activities

Accommodation, Eating and Drinking Services

Note: p.p.: percentage points. Seasonally adjusted.
Source: Ministry of Health, Labour and Welfare, Monthly Labour Survey.

The pandemic also amplified a negative trend in hours worked in Japan. Throughout 2019 hours worked had been declining, varying between 0.4 and 4.4 percentage points less than the same period in 2018 (Figure 1.11). In May 2019 hours worked dropped by 4.4 percentage points and there was a further decrease of 9.3% in May 2020. The government expanded employment subsidies which allowed employers to put workers on temporary leave while keeping them employed. As a reaction to the sharp decline in consumer demand, worker hours were reduced. Overtime work was drastically reduced to offset the decrease in demand, but there were also reductions in scheduled working hours per day and reduced number of workdays. The reduction in working hours were particularly prominent for those who worked more than 50 hours pre-pandemic, women, workers living in Tokyo and Kansai region and service-intense industries (Takami, 2021[12]).

Figure 1.11. The COVID-19 crisis intensified an already negative trend in hours worked

Average hours worked, year on year

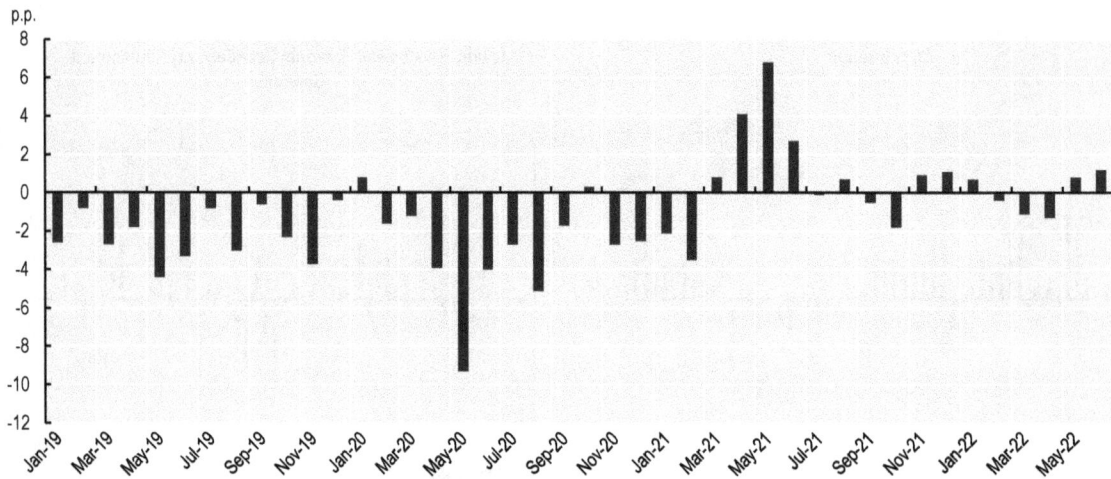

Note: p.p.: percentage points. Ration to the same period of the preceding year.
Source: Ministry of Health, Labour and Welfare, Monthly Labour Survey.

1.3. The skills composition of the Japanese labour force and its evolution during the pandemic

1.3.1. Skills imbalances were rising in the Japanese labour market prior to the pandemic

Prior to the pandemic, both labour shortages and hiring mismatch were on the rise in Japan (OECD, 2021[13]). The effective job-opening ratio, an indicator of how many jobs are available relative to the total number of job seekers registered at the public employment service (Hello Work), hit a 45-year high in 2018. At the same time the relationship between the unemployment rate and the vacancy rate – the so-called Beveridge Curve – indicated that despite an increase in vacancies, there was no decrease in unemployment, suggesting mismatch. Many companies faced difficulties in recruiting workers with the right vocational skills, with 53% of companies reporting difficulties in attracting skilled workers already in the labour force due to difficulties in hiring motivated young and mid-career workers. A further 88% of employers faced talent shortages, much higher than the OECD average of 53% (OECD, 2021[13]).

Skills shortages in Japan were also evident in the OECD Skills for Jobs indicators. The indicators showed that shortages were most intensive in security occupations, construction and mining occupations and transport and machine operation occupations. The Japanese skill shortages differed from the average for OECD countries. The OECD average had a concentration of skill shortages in high-qualified occupations, with shortages in reading comprehension, writing and critical thinking. For Japan, the largest skill shortages were found in technical skills such as repair, operation monitoring and equipment maintenance, which are skills associated with low and middle-skilled occupations. Comparatively, these technical skills were in surplus in the OECD average. It should be noted, however, that a surplus of a certain skill does not mean that this skill is not needed in the labour market, but only that the supply exceeds the demand.

Data from the Survey of Adult Skills (PIAAC) show that the skills for workers are not always put to full use at work, meaning that, although employed Japanese adults have high literacy and numeracy proficiency, the intensity of use of these skills is lower than in many other OECD countries (OECD, 2021[13]). There is also a substantial gap in skills use between men and women, as well as between full-time and part-time workers, for both literacy and numeracy skills.

1.3.2. A diverse range of skills are present in the Japanese labour market

A previous report by the OECD provided an overview of skills developments in Japan based on PIAAC data collected in 2012 (OECD, 2021[13]). The Japanese economy has since undergone considerable changes, both in terms of skill requirements within occupations and in terms of the occupational composition of the labour force. Therefore, in order to capture the current skills make-up of the Japanese labour market, there is a need to incorporate newer data. In an effort to use more recent labour market data and a Japan-specific skill taxonomy, this report innovatively combines two new databases – the recently released Japanese O*NET database (called "job tag") by the Japan Institute for Labour Policy and Training and the Japanese Panel Study of Employment Dynamics (JPSED) published by the Recruit Works Institute – to paint a clearer picture of current skills composition and developments in Japan. Details on the two datasets and how they were merged can be found in Box 1.1.

Box 1.1. Measuring skills in Japanese data

Understanding occupational skills

Despite the key role skills play in societies and economies, there is little agreement in the literature as to what "skills" are and how they should be defined. The term "skill" can refer to generic cognitive (e.g. reasoning or remembering) and non-cognitive abilities (e.g. teamwork or self-organisation) as well as to skills that are specific to a particular job, occupation or sector (e.g. accounting or hair colouring) (OECD, 2016[14]). The great number of empirical studies on skills reflects the many ways that skills have been approximated in the literature and, as such, highlights the difficulty of coming up with a shared definition of what skills are or a good proxy or indicator for measuring them (see OECD (2017[15]) for analysis of previous literature on skills).

Most studies of skill requirements undertaken internationally rely on the United States O*NET database, under the assumption that its content is relevant to other countries (Bruns, Evans and Luque, 2012[16]; Frey and Osborne, 2017[17]). The O*NET database describes the skills, abilities and knowledge required in each occupation by defining the level at which they are used, and their importance. However, the O*NET database has been constructed gathering information on the tasks and skills that are part of occupations in the United States. Adopting this data for other countries is possible under the assumption that occupations have the same skill requirements, irrespective of country characteristics such as the level of digitalisation at work or the type of technologies and tools that are available in local labour markets i.e. truck drivers in the United States uses the same level of skills as truck drivers in Germany. Though this might be true for countries with a similar economic structure and level of development as the United States, the American O*NET may not be an appropriate measure of skill requirements in very different labour markets as is the case of Japan. First, in Japan, the practice of life-long employment can be a barrier for horizontal skill transfers between employers, meaning that the responsibility of post-education skills investment falls on the company – a fact evident by the lack of private adult learning opportunities outside the company. Secondly, as the Japanese economy relies heavily on internal training for career purposes, there is a risk that skills requirements are more firm-specific and are not as transversal as in an economy with more horizontal movement of workers between firms, such as the United States. Finally, a large share of Japanese companies are small and medium-sized enterprises (SMEs). SMEs tend to invest less in training of their workforce than larger enterprises (OECD, 2021[18]), and this may yield different skill requirements at work.[1]

"Job tag"

To facilitate the practice of career education in schools, job hunting for job seekers, and recruiting activities of companies in Japan, Ministry of Health, Labour and Welfare launched a new website "job tag" in 2020. Four types of information are currently available: text-based descriptions, cross-occupational numeric estimates, recent labour market information, and visual content (short videos). The source of the first two types of information is the database called "input data" developed by the Japan Institute for Labour Policy and Training (JILPT). The domains and items of cross-occupational numeric estimates are basically derived from US O*NET, "job tag" contains a taxonomy of skills, knowledge, work context and work activities, and it measures their level or importance in each occupations. The taxonomy is standardised so that every occupation has a value for every skill, ranging from 0 if the skill is not used in that occupation to 7 if it is required at high levels. The levels have been determined through surveying workers in the different occupations. After conducting interviews with career consultants starting in June 2018 and individual industries (IT, manufacturing) starting in October 2018, workers surveys were conducted in December 2018 and November 2019 (about 50 workers on average per occupation) to compile quantitative data for about 500 occupations (The Japan Institute for Labour Policy and Training, 2020[19]). Thereafter, about 10 new occupations will be added each year.

The occupations listed in "job tag" are intended to cover existing occupations in a systematic and comprehensive manner. However, since the design of the database is focused on being useful to career consultants and corporate human resource personnel who provide employment assistance, occupations that use these services less (e.g. professional sports players and artists) are not included (The Japan Institute for Labour Policy and Training, 2021[20]).

To understand the advantages of the "job tag" data, it is first crucial to understand the relationship between skills and tasks, and how tasks can be taken as proxies for skills. Acemoglu and Author (2010[21]) define a task as a "unit of work activity that produces output (goods and services)", while a skill is "a worker's endowment of capabilities for performing various tasks". As workers apply their skills to perform tasks and those tasks produce an output, we accept that one skill can perform several tasks, and a worker can change the set of tasks they perform in response to changes in labour market conditions and technology while still using the same set of skills. If a task (or a group of similar tasks) is performed less and less over a given time period, it is inferred that the corresponding skill (or skills) needed to carry out that task is less present in the labour market.

The Japan Institute for Labour Policy and Training defines skills, work context and work activities as following (The Japan Institute for Labour Policy and Training, 2020[19]):

- **Skills:** Occupational skills refer to "the acquired ability of an individual to perform work". In other words, among the individual abilities of being able to do this kind of work, the abilities that can be accumulated and improved through practice and training are vocational skills. Skills here is a quantification of the standard skill requirements for the performance of duties. There are 35 skills items that are similar to the US O*NET skill areas (39 items).

- **Work Context:** The nature (characteristics) of the activities performed at work and the environment surrounding them can be described from various perspectives. For example, the need for teamwork (interpersonal relationships), whether the work is done indoors or outdoors (physical environment), and the extent to which individuals are allowed discretion in their work (structural characteristics). The "Work Context" information area shows the standard situation for each occupation in terms of these information. "Job tag" is mainly based on the US O*NET (categorised into 57 elements) with some localisation, and 37 elements are currently available (most of them were answered by workers on a 5-point scale), though at the time of the analysis only 23 were developed (the rest were added in 2022). The reason why the number of work context elements is less than half that of the US O*NET is to reduce the burden on survey respondents, and was determined based on the opinions of career consultants and other factors.

- **Work activities:** Work activities, like Generalised Work Activities (GWA) in the US O*NET, are an accumulation of similar underlying job activities and job actions in fulfilling major work roles. While the US O*NET lists "importance" and "level," "job tag" collects only "importance" – a survey design decision intended to reduce survey response time for participants and make it easier to compare the different elements.

Creating a time-varying database to measure the skills composition of the Japanese workforce using the Japanese Panel Study on Employment Dynamics (JPSED) survey

As the "job tag" database presents a static snapshot of skills used in different occupations, it needs to be merged with time-varying labour market data source to capture change in the skill composition of the workforce over the years. For the purpose of this report, the JPSED survey, published by the Recruit Works Institute, was used. The survey, carried out between 2016 and 2021, contains responses from approximately 60 000 people per year in Japan on various topics related to the labour market. The survey was merged with "job tag" by matching at the occupation level using a cross-walk developed by the OECD. As the JPSED survey contains 223 occupations (excluding unclassified) while "job tag" contains approximately 500 occupations, some occupations were matched directly (such as the occupation named "aestheticians" in JPSED and the occupation named "aestheticians" in "job tag", while some occupations in "job tag" were combined to create an "umbrella" occupation that more closely matched that in JPSED (such as the occupations "Japanese cuisine cook", "sushi chef" and "soba and udon cook" in "job tag" which have been all merged and matched with "Japanese cooks and sushi chefs" in JPSED).

1. This does not mean, however, that the skills differ across countries, just the levels. This is also reflected in the way O*NET surveys are set up – each occupation has the same list of skills just at a different level, e.g. both data scientist and cleaner will have the skill "programming", but the data scientist will have a much higher level for that skill than the cleaner. When comparing US O*NET and "job tag" these differences become evident. For example, one of the key skills of a psychiatrist is social perceptiveness/understanding of other people's reactions, which has a high level in both the "job tag" and US O*NET (5.2 for the former and 5.3 in the latter out of 7). However, due to the differences in how psychiatrists conduct their work, Japanese psychiatrists require a level of 4.4 for the skill "co-ordinating with others", while American psychiatrist only require a level of 3.8 for the same skill, possibly due to the high rate of psychiatrists working on in-patient treatment relative to the United States.

By combining data from the JPSED and "job tag", it is possible to construct an indicator to represent the skills composition of the Japanese workforce.[2] This indicator is calculated as a weighted average, using the employment share of each occupation as a weight – in other words, the score of each skill used in each occupation – a value that ranges between 0 and 7 – is multiplied by the number of employed people in the occupation based on the JPSED, and then dividing that by the total number of employed people. The result is that each skill gets a value between 0 and 7 that shows how prevalent that skill is in the workforce. For a skill to have a high value, it will need to be required in many large occupations – occupations that employ many people. If a skill has a low value, this can be because: i) it is only required at a low level for any occupation; ii) it is required at a high level for some occupations but those occupations employ relatively few people; or iii) a mix of the two.

Figure 1.12 summarises the skills composition of the Japanese workforce in 2021. The results show that foundational skills – i.e. those skills that are the building block for a lifelong learning such as listening comprehension, explanatory skills, reading comprehension and writing skills – are most present in the labour market. Figure 1.13 show that these are the dominant skills even in occupations in Japan that require them the least – i.e. the minimum requirement for reading, writing, listening and explaining is relatively high. A high level of foundational skills is an indicator of a knowledge-based economy with a highly qualified labour force, where most jobs (both physical and analytical) requires the worker to engage in relative high levels of reading, writing, speaking and listening. It is therefore hardly surprising that in a modern highly-developed economy such as Japan that many occupations require a high level of foundational skills.

In addition to foundational skills, high levels of social skills are also important. Social skills measure the level at which different social interactions are required at work – e.g. guidance, understanding of other people's reactions, co-ordinating with others, persuasion, negotiation and ongoing observation and evaluation. Most jobs in the Japanese workforce require a relative high level of social skills, still the value of the top percentiles for social skills are lower than for foundational skills. Social skills are increasing in prominence in the labour market, as repetitive and routine tasks are automated. A US study shows that workers who possess both high social and technical skills experience better employment prospects and wages, compared with those who only have high technical skills (Deming, 2017[22]). A relatively high level of social skills in Japan in 2021 reflects many people working in occupations where work tasks require a moderate to high level of social skills, whereas there are few occupations currently that require a very high level of social skills.

Advance cognitive skills are central to solving non-routine problems and managing non-routine situations, and are key in a world of rapid changes and uncertainty. The requirement of advanced cognitive skills indicates how complex tasks are. However, for the time being, advanced cognitive skills are relatively less present in the Japanese workforce. While complex problem solving and critical thinking rank mid-tier in Japan, rational decision making ranks low in the skills composition list.

Technical skills such as requirement analysis, selection of tools and installation and configuration score in the middle to low end of the scale. Figure 1.13 shows that there are very few occupations that require high levels of technical skills, as the median is low. Since the calculation is a weighted average of the level of skills for an occupation and the share of people working in that occupation, it is possible that technical skills rank low because there are not many people working in the few occupations that require technical skills. This may reflect the structure of the Japanese economy or suggest a difficulty in finding workers with the required technical skills. The latter would be in line with the shortage in technical skills found in the OECD Skills for Jobs Indicators.

At the bottom of the list are reading, writing, speaking and listening skills related to foreign languages. This may reflect that Japanese companies put a limited premium on foreign language skills and therefore the occupations use foreign language skills less. This does not, however, reflect the actual level of language skills in the society, just the skills presence in the carrying out of job-related tasks. It is still worth noting that (if excluding the skill 'repair') foreign language has the lowest maximum value of all skills in the Japanese labour market.

Overall, the analysis of minimum, maximum and mean values shows a more 'normal' distribution for skills with a high frequency – meaning the mean is approximately halfway between the minimum and maximum values – and a distribution skewed towards low values for skills with a low frequency. This is likely due to very few workers in occupations of high value of low-frequency skills.

Figure 1.12. The skills composition of the Japanese workforce is very diverse

Skills composition indicator (scale 1-7)

Skill level

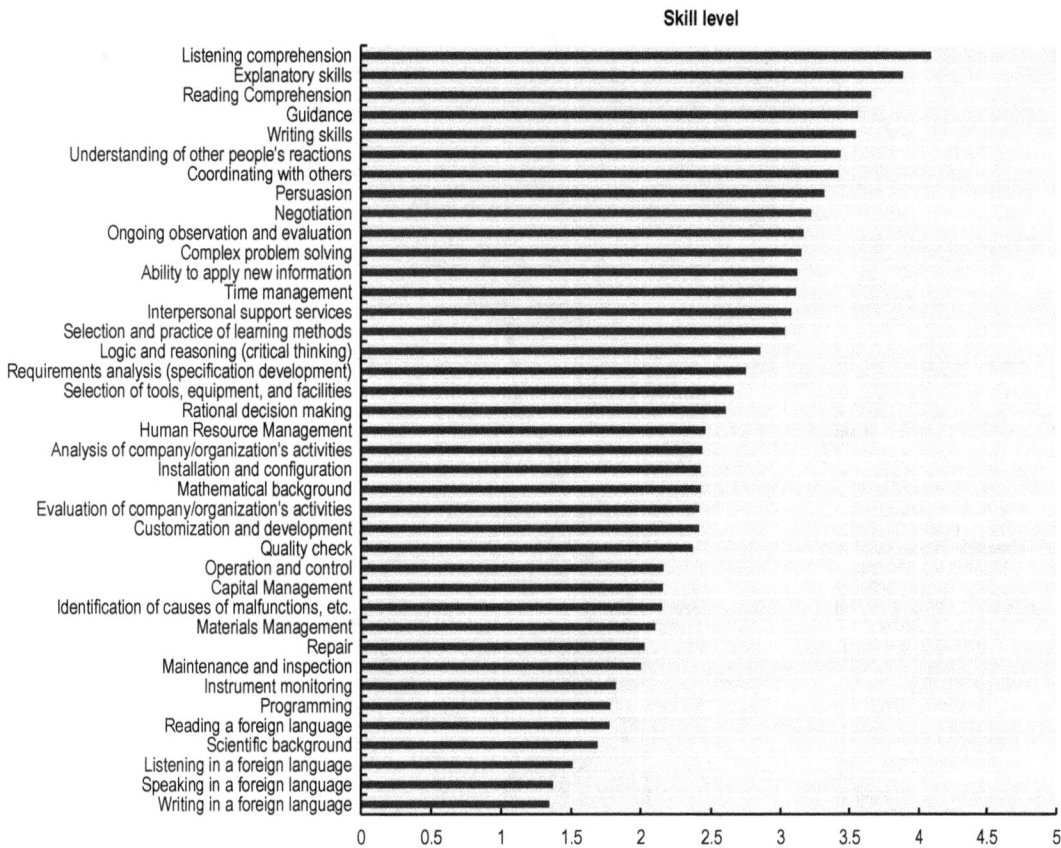

Note: The Skills Composition Indicator is calculated using a weighted average, taking into account both skill level of occupation and number of people working in that occupation, and it is calculated by multiplying each skill level for a given occupation with the number of workers in that occupation, and then dividing by the total number of workers in the data set. The sample includes employees between 20 and 65 years old. The full scale for skill level ranges from 0 to 7, but has been shortened to 0-5 to better present the data.
Source: Japanese Panel Study of Employment Dynamics and "job tag".

Figure 1.13. Foundational skills have higher minimum value than technical skills because they are needed for almost every job in the Japanese economy

Minimum and maximum level for each skill and the weighted mean

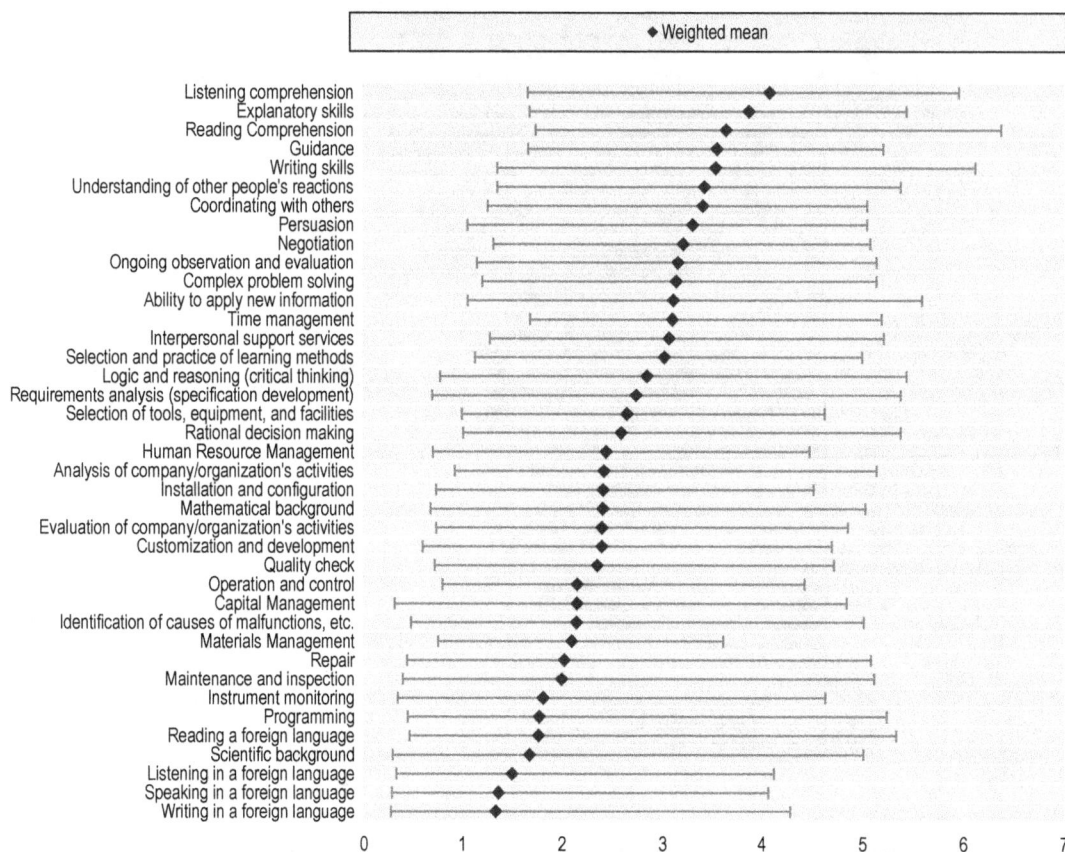

Note: The weighted mean is calculated using a weighted average, taking into account both skill level of occupation and number of people working in that occupation, and it is calculated by multiplying each skill level for a given occupation with the number of workers in that occupation, and then dividing by the total number of workers in the data set. Minimum/maximum value refers to occupation with the lowest/highest value in the dataset. 50th percentile shows the value at which 50% of the population score equal or less than. The sample includes employees between 20 and 65 years old. The scale for skill level ranges from 0 to 7, but has been shortened to 0-5 to better present the data.
Source: Japanese Panel Study of Employment Dynamics and "job tag".

1.3.3. The skills composition of the Japanese workforce is evolving

Across most OECD countries, substantial changes in skill needs are challenging labour market and training policies and contributing to skill mismatch and shortages. In general, social and analytical skills are on the rise while many countries are experiencing a declining demand of manual skills (Nedelkoska and Quintini, 2018[23]). The skills composition of Japan is in constant evolution. Table 1.1 shows the results of estimating changes in skill requirements over time, while controlling for changes in the age structure and the gender structure of the working population – two social indicators that have seen large changes in the Japanese labour market in recent years. To compare with the findings in the literature, indicators for social and analytical skills have been constructed (see Box 1.2 for details).

Econometric results using individual-level data point to a significant upward trend in the incidence of social skills and abilities in Japan, with much of this increase occurring during the pandemic. Indeed, a positive increase in social skills and social work contexts can be observed in all years (though less intensely in 2020), with 2021 showing a particularly large increase in comparison to the other years. By contrast, analytical skills requirements in the Japanese workforce remained quite stable over time, except for a significant jump in 2021. Pre-pandemic studies using German and UK data show a similar trend for social skills, although they also show a consistent increase in analytical skill requirements (Nedelkoska and Quintini, 2018[23]). Overall, the analysis on Japan indicates that the pandemic has increased the speed at which the labour market is moving towards more social and analytical skills. As we are not able to observe changes within occupations, this is a reflection of a change in the structure of employment in the context of the pandemic. For example, the increase in intensity could be due to a shift in the labour market towards jobs that can be carried out remotely through teleworking. It remains to be seen if this increase is structural will be sustained after the pandemic.

Table 1.1. Social skills have increased significantly in Japan while the pandemic has accelerated the shift in both social and analytical skills

Marginal effects of the change in social skills, social work contexts and analytical skills, 2017-2021

	Social skills	Social work contexts	Analytical skills
2018 dummy	0.006	0.006	0.000
	(0.003)*	(0.003)	(0.002)
2019 dummy	0.007	0.01	-0.001
	(0.003)*	(0.003)**	(0.003)
2020 dummy	0.006	0.006	-0.002
	(0.003)	(0.003)	(0.003)
2021 dummy	0.013	0.014	0.006
	(0.003)**	(0.003)**	(0.002)*
Female	-0.15	0.042	-0.246
	(0.004)**	(0.006)**	(0.005)**
Age	0.002	0.001	0.003
	(0.000)**	(0.000)**	(0.000)**
N	175 168	175 168	175 168

Note: The sample includes employees between 20 and 65 years old. Marginal effects estimated from the results of logit models. Standard errors clustered by prefecture in parentheses. Significant at: *** $p<0.01$, ** $p<0.05$, * $p<0.1$.
Source: JPSED 2017-21.

Table 1.2 shows the results of estimating key indicators for manual skills,[3] using the same specifications as for analytical skills, social skills and social work contexts. For all three indicators an increase can be observed in all years, though the intensity of the increase drops significantly in 2021. This could be due to the physical restrictions implemented during the pandemic, where carrying out physical tasks became difficult while observing strict lockdown and social distancing rules. More data is needed to evaluate whether this slowdown in the rate of increase is a temporary reaction to restrictions or if the pandemic has permanently slowed the rise in importance of manual skills in the Japan workforce, but previous analysis on manual skills in Japan have yielded similar results (Handel, 2012[24])

Table 1.2. Manual skills are still increasing in Japan, though less intensely than before the pandemic

Marginal effects of the change in indicators of manual skills, 2017-2021

	Manual handling of objects, tools and controls	Use of whole body to carry out physical activities	Use of hands and arms to handle and move objects
2018 dummy	0.008	0.013	0.008
	(0.002)**	(0.003)**	(0.002)**
2019 dummy	0.015	0.013	0.015
	(0.003)**	(0.003)**	(0.003)**
2020 dummy	0.018	0.013	0.019
	(0.004)**	(0.004)**	(0.003)**
2021 dummy	0.009	0.007	0.011
	(0.004)*	(0.004)	(0.004)**
Female	-0.005	-0.102	0.002
	(0.007)	(0.007)**	(0.008)
Age	-0.005	-0.001	-0.005
	(0.000)**	(0.000)**	(0.000)**
N	175581	175581	175581

Note: The sample includes employees between 20 and 65 years old. Marginal effects estimated from the results of logit models. Standard errors clustered by prefecture in parentheses. Significant at: *** $p<0.01$, ** $p<0.05$, * $p<0.1$.
Source: JPSED 2017-21.

Box 1.2. Calculation of changes in social, analytical and manual skills

Social and analytical indices

In order to understand how the demand for social and analytical skills has evolved in Japan in the last five years – between 2017 and 2021 – three variables are created for the purpose of the analysis:

- Analytical skills equals 1 if at least one of the following variables scored in the top tercile for that skill: complex problem solving, logic and reasoning (critical thinking) or rational decision making. Otherwise it equals 0.
- Social skills equals 1 if at least one of the following variables scored in the top tercile for that skill: understanding of other people's reaction, persuasion and negotiation. Otherwise it equals 0.
- Social work contexts equals 1 if at least one of the following variables scored in the top tercile for that work context: interacting with others, working in a group or team or co-ordinating and learning with others. Otherwise it equals 0.

Skill demands in the three skills and one work context are then estimated as a function of time. The reference year is taken to be 2017 and skill demand in 2018, 2019, 2020 and 2021 is expressed as difference relative to the reference year. Logit models are estimated since the four skills/work contexts are defined as binary variables. The variables of interest are the year dummies (2018-21), while 2017 is the reference year against which the trend is estimated.

Manual skills

Calculating the skill trends in manual work is made more complicated as the indicators for manual work are not categorised under the same category in "job tag" and hence the respondents have not answered the questions using the same scale. Therefore we cannot construct a dummy variable for manual work. However, three binary variables are created for the purpose of analysing trends in manual work:

- Manual handling of objects, tools and controls equals 1 if this skill is scored in the top tercile for that occupation. Otherwise it equals 0.
- Use the whole body to carry out physical activities equals 1 if this skill is scored in the top tercile for that occupation. Otherwise it equals 0.
- Use hands and arms to handle and move objects equals 1 if this skill is scored in the top tercile for that occupation. Otherwise it equals 0.

For both the social and analytical indices and manual skills, the estimates are done at the individual level.

Key takeaways

Reductions in wages and working hours have helped Japan to dampen falls in employment and rises in unemployment during the COVID-19 crisis relative to many other OECD countries. However, a small number of industries and some socio-economic groups have borne the brunt of the pandemic's employment impact, particularly women and non-regular workers, and those working the accommodation and living-service sector.

Analysis of the Japanese labour market prior to the pandemic shows that skills mismatches had been emerging for some time. Employers found it increasingly difficult to fill vacancies due to the lack of appropriate skills in the labour market, and the OECD's Skills for Jobs indicators showed that, in contrast to the OECD average, shortages were concentrated in technical skills. An analysis of the current skill composition of the Japanese workforce shows that fundamental and social skills are most present in the labour market, while technical skills and foreign languages are less present. Advance cognitive skills, a good indicator for complex work tasks that cannot easily be automated, are perhaps less present in Japan than might be expected.

Looking at trends over time, there has been an increase in social and analytical skills, especially during the pandemic, while the growth rate of manual skills has tapered off – indicating that the Japanese labour market is experiencing many of the same trends as in other OECD countries.

Annex 1.A. Additional data

Annex Figure 1.A.1. Effects on wages by year, employment type and sex

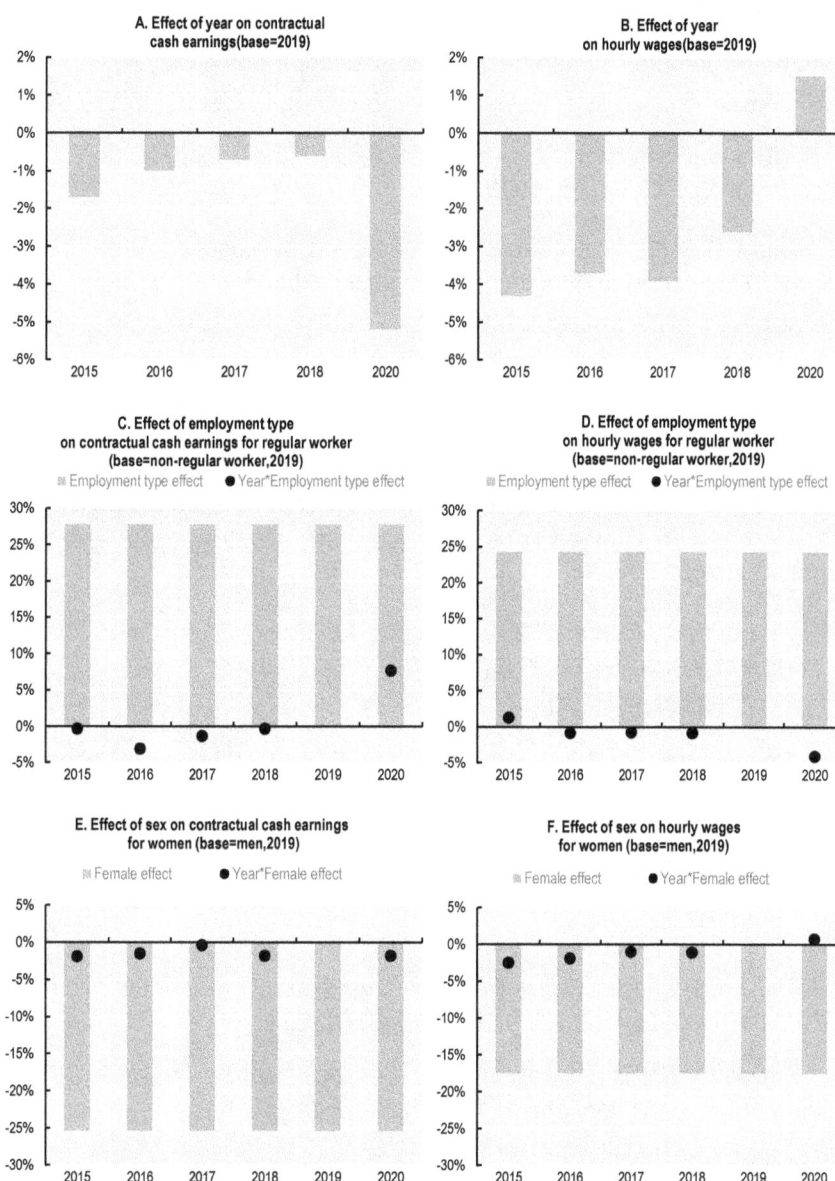

Note: The panels show estimates of the impact of selected variables on wages for workers other than part time workers and temporary workers. Hourly wages means the contractual cash earnings divided by the sum of scheduled working hours and overtime working hours. The base year is 2019. Wage effects are estimated controlling for variables such as year, sex, employment type, firm size, industry, education, age, age-squared, years of service, and years of service-squared using a log-linear regression. The effects in the panels are the coefficients obtained from the regressions. Panels C and D show the effect using the interaction term for year and employment type, and Panel E and F show the effect using the interaction term for year and sex. For Panels A, B, D and F, all variables above are statistically significant at 1%. For Panel C, the interaction terms of regular worker and 2015, and regular worker and 2018 are not significant, while the others are statistically significant at 1%. For Panel E, the interaction term of women and 2017 is statistically significant at 5%, while the others are statistically significant at 1%.
Source: OECD analysis based on Basic Survey on Wage Structure supported by the Ministry of Health, Labour and Welfare.

References

Acemoglu, D. and D. Autor (2010), "Skills, Tasks and Technologies: Implications for Employment and Earnings", *National Bureau of Economic Research Working Paper Series* 1682. [21]

Bruns, B., D. Evans and J. Luque (2012), "Achieving World-Class Education in Brazil : The Next Agenda.", *World Bank - Directions in Development*. [16]

Cabinet Office (2020), "Emergency Economic Measures to Cope with COVID-19", https://www5.cao.go.jp/keizai1/keizaitaisaku/2020/20200420_economic_measures.pdf. [1]

Deming, D. (2017), "The Growing Importance of Social Skills in the Labor Market", *The Quarterly Journal of Economics*, Vol. 132/4, pp. 1593-1640, https://doi.org/10.1093/QJE/QJX022. [22]

Frey, C. and M. Osborne (2017), "The future of employment: How susceptible are jobs to computerisation?", *Technological Forecasting and Social Change*, Vol. 114, pp. 254-280, https://doi.org/10.1016/j.techfore.2016.08.019. [17]

Handel, M. (2012), "Trends in Job Skill Demands in OECD Countries", *OECD Social, Employment and Migration Working Papers* No. 143, https://doi.org/10.1787/5k8zk8pcq6td-en (accessed on 23 May 2022). [24]

Leussink, D. (2021), "Japan real wages eke out first rise in a year as COVID-19 hits prices", *Reuters*, https://www.reuters.com/article/us-japan-economy-wages-idUSKBN2BS25S (accessed on 15 April 2022). [11]

Ministry of Health, Labour and Welfare (2022), "Effective Job Openings for Child Care Workers (Nationwide) "保育士の有効求人倍率の推移(全国)"", https://www.mhlw.go.jp/content/R2.11..pdf. [10]

Ministry of Land, Infrastructure, Transport and Tourism (2021), *2021 Tourism White Paper*, https://www.mlit.go.jp/statistics/content/001408958.pdf. [3]

Nedelkoska, L. and G. Quintini (2018), "Automation, skills use and training", *OECD Social, Employment and Migration Working Papers*, No. 202, OECD Publishing, Paris, https://doi.org/10.1787/2e2f4eea-en. [23]

OECD (2021), *Creating Responsive Adult Learning Opportunities in Japan*, Getting Skills Right, OECD Publishing, Paris, https://doi.org/10.1787/cfe1ccd2-en. [13]

OECD (2021), *Incentives for SMEs to Invest in Skills: Lessons from European Good Practices*, OECD Publishing, Paris, https://doi.org/10.1787/1eb16dc7-en. [18]

OECD (2021), *OECD Economic Surveys: Japan 2021*, OECD Publishing, Paris, https://doi.org/10.1787/6b749602-en. [5]

OECD (2021), *OECD Employment Outlook 2021: Navigating the COVID-19 Crisis and Recovery*, OECD Publishing, Paris, https://doi.org/10.1787/5a700c4b-en. [7]

OECD (2021), *OECD Quarterly Employment Situation 3rd Quarter 2021*, https://www.oecd.org/sdd/labour-stats/employment-situation-oecd-01-2022.pdf (accessed on 7 April 2022). [4]

OECD (2020), *OECD Employment Outlook 2020: Worker Security and the COVID-19 Crisis*, [2]
OECD Publishing, Paris, https://doi.org/10.1787/1686c758-en.

OECD (2017), *Getting Skills Right: Skills for Jobs Indicators*, Getting Skills Right, OECD [15]
Publishing, Paris, https://doi.org/10.1787/9789264277878-en.

OECD (2016), *Getting Skills Right: Assessing and Anticipating Changing Skill Needs*, Getting [14]
Skills Right, OECD Publishing, Paris, https://doi.org/10.1787/9789264252073-en.

OECD (2015), *In It Together: Why Less Inequality Benefits All* (Summary in Japanese), [8]
https://doi.org/10.1787/26d81e2b-ja.

Shibata, H. (2017), "A Study of Non-Regular Employees in Japan: Focus on Female Part- [9]
Timers", *Senshu Journal of Human Sciences, Sociology*, Vol. Vol. 7/No. 2, pp. pp.025-042,
https://senshu-
u.repo.nii.ac.jp/?action=pages_view_main&active_action=repository_view_main_item_detail&
item_id=4351&item_no=1&page_id=13&block_id=21 (accessed on 7 April 2022).

Takami, T. (2021), "Working Hours under the COVID-19 Pandemic in Japan: Reviewing [12]
Changes by Situation Phase during and after the 2020 State of Emergency Declaration",
Japan Labor Issues, Vol. 5/30, https://www.jil.go.jp/english/jli/documents/2021/030-01.pdf
(accessed on 10 March 2022).

The Japan Institute for Labour Policy and Training (2021), "Study on the Development of Input [20]
Data for the Occupational Information Providing Website (Japanese version of O*NET)(職業
情報提供サイト（日本版 O-NET）のインプットデータ開発に関する研究（2020年度）",
https://www.jil.go.jp/institute/siryo/2021/documents/240.pdf.

The Japan Institute for Labour Policy and Training (2020), *Study on the Development of Input* [19]
*Data for the Occupational Information Providing Website (Japanese version of O*NET)(職業*
情報提供サイト（日本版O-NET）のインプットデータ開発に関する研究).

Yamaguchi, K. (2019), "Gender Inequalities in the Japanese Workplace and Employment", [6]
Springer - Advances in Japanese Business and Economics, Vol. 22,
http://www.springer.com/series/11682 (accessed on 20 April 2022).

Notes

[1] However, these large falls partly reflect a difference in the statistical treatment of workers on short-term lay-off: In North America, these workers are counted as unemployed rather than as still employed as in some other countries.

[2] Bruns, Evans and Luque, 2012[15] calculate skills composition in Brazil and the United States by using US O*NET and combining it with Brazilian and American labour force surveys (*Perquisa Nacional por Amostragem de Domicilios*, US Census and the American Community survey,) under the assumption that US O*NET is an appropriate reference scheme for the Brazilian labour market. The authors estimate skills composite by income quantile using five indices comprised of underlying skills, as defined by Acemoglu and Autor, 2010[18]. The result shows average indices scores by income quantiles, as well as percentage of occupations in which the undelying indices skills are considered important or very important. This method has two drawbacks: i) the analysis of skill indicies as opposed to direct skills does not allow for an analysis of importance of certain skills over others, and ii) by focusing on the highest scoring occupations it does not accurately present the presence of skills in the labour market. Therefore, the analysis for Japan will take into account all skills at all values to present a complete overview of skills in the economy.

[3] Refer to Box 1.2 for details on the construction of the indicators for manual skills.

2 The policy response of the Japanese Government during the pandemic

Japan's response to the pandemic has been prompt and wide-ranging. This chapter provides an overview of policies in three main areas related to the labour market: employment subsidies, online career guidance and teleworking. The chapter summarises the main challenges and responses and provides international comparisons and best-practice. The chapter also explores how digitalisation of public services and increase in remote work modes have improved flexibilities for some while increasing inequalities for others. Finally, the chapter provides direction on how to further tailor and improve these policies to build a resilient and sustainable labour market.

In Brief

Japan needs to strengthen skills policies and foster digitalisation in order to respond to future challenges

In the early stages of the COVID-19 outbreak, the Japanese Government placed particular emphasis on individual job retention schemes, with a widening of economic support for individuals who were no longer able to work or had their working hours reduced. The interventions were largely successful in preventing a substantial increase in unemployment; however, they were costly. In addition to job retention schemes, the Japanese Government accelerated the digital delivery of public services, including the digitalisation of career guidance. Existing career guidance services were moved online, so that they could be accessed during times of confinement and social distancing. On the positive side, the digitalisation of services has addressed pre-existing obstacles to training participation such as time constraints, by increasing the flexibility in access and usage. However, survey data shows that the uptake of digital career guidance remains low for some groups, and it is vital that Japan ensures sufficient digital infrastructure and digital skills for those who risk falling behind in the digital transformation.

Moreover, public authorities have also encouraged the modernisation of work practices through the promotion of telework. The uptake of teleworking practices has been considerable in Japan during the COVID-19 pandemic. This has contributed to changing attitudes towards teleworking, with the practice being more favourably viewed by both employers and workers who have experienced teleworking. However, employers who put emphasis on overtime work and working during holidays have been more conservative in adopting teleworking practices. There is also a growing gap in teleworking practices between the "traditional" employees and those with less favourable labour market conditions, further exacerbating disparities.

As the level of economic activity returns to normal, the cornerstone of employment measures will need to shift from maintaining employment (which has been costly) to supporting the skills development of a heterogeneous labour force to better exploit their abilities. In this context, fostering the digitalisation of career guidance services and promoting teleworking practices will be key. It will also be important to ensure that support measures are inclusive of workers who have been strongly affected by COVID-19, such as low-skilled workers and non-regular workers.

2.1. Measures implemented to support employment retention in response to COVID-19

As discussed in the previous chapter, the negative employment impact of the COVID-19 pandemic was most severe for non-regular workers and women as well as in specific sectors. Under these circumstances, conventional employment support measures – such as employment insurance or regular public vocational training – were not sufficient to support those most in need, and the Japanese Government created and expanded various programmes, including employment adjustment subsidies and a new payment scheme for workers in SMEs and workers whose working days are not set in advance and who were forced to take leave from work by employers because of the COVID-19 situation and not able to receive leave allowances. In the fiscal year 2020, the scale of Japan's mitigation and recovery measures in response to the COVID-19 pandemic was about 54% of GDP, higher than in the United States (31%), United Kingdom (32%), and France (28%) (Cabinet Office, 2022[1]).[1]

Part of Japan's training measures were also implemented through the employment subsidies, as Japan was one of the few countries where some level of training subsidies has traditionally been integrated into its job retention scheme. By reskilling workers while employees were out of work, firms could receive a supplementary payment in addition to the regular employment adjustment subsidy. This system can be viewed as a way of having companies provide training to respond to the shift in Japan's overall industrial structure as part of the firms' internal employment retention system, instead of the government providing the training. As such, this system is in line with the specific features of the Japanese labour market, where it is common for workers to be assigned to various jobs within the same company at the request of their employers. As will be discussed below, this system of education and training as a job retention scheme was expanded after the outbreak of the COVID-19 pandemic.

2.1.1. Employment adjustment subsidies played a key role in supporting job retention

The Ministry of Labour has been offering employment adjustment subsidies (*Koyo Chosei Joseikin*) since 1975. These are a special type of subsidies aimed at maintaining worker's employment when firms are forced to reduce their business activities. Prior to the outbreak of COVID-19, this subsidy was available to employers whose sales dropped by 10% or more in the last three months compared with the previous year, and had to send at least one worker on leave (in accordance with a specific labour-management agreement) (Table 2.1). The amount of the subsidies was capped at JPY 8 370 per day, and the subsidy rate was two-thirds of the worker's wages for SMEs and one-half for large companies. Workers eligible for the subsidy were limited to those covered by employment insurance, and the maximum number of days of payment was set at 100 days per year.

Immediately after the outbreak of the COVID-19 pandemic, the Japanese Government eased the requirements for accessing the employment adjustment subsidy, increased the subsidy rate, and raised the maximum subsidy payment. The government also expanded the programme to provide benefits to part-time workers and other groups that were not eligible for employment insurance and therefore were previously not eligible for the subsidy. A system was established to provide benefits directly to workers in small and medium-sized enterprises (SMEs) and workers whose working days are not set in advance and who were forced to take leave from work by employers because of the COVID-19 situation and not able to receive leave allowances during its period. Compared to the approach taken by the Japanese authorities during the 2008 financial crisis, the COVID-19 measures innovatively focused on vulnerable groups such as non-regular workers and workers in SMEs.

The government also doubled the subsidy rate covering education and training leave (from the original amount of JPY 1 200 per day to JPY 2 400 for SMEs and JPY 1 800 for other companies). These amounts were paid in addition to the subsidies for absence from work. While workers were previously not allowed to work on the day of the training in order to receive this subsidy, after COVID-19 the revised system allows them to work part-time, as long as the training was at least three hours per day. Moreover, the programme has been expanded to those adults undertaking their training online at home or undertaking training for non-vocational skills such as business etiquette training and mental health training. Firms were able to receive this additional subsidy by submitting documents describing the content of the education and training, training plan, and documents certifying that the worker has completed the training.

Table 2.1. Employment and training subsidies were greatly expanded in response to COVID-19

	Before COVID-19	After COVID-19
Requirements	Sales decreased by 10% or more in the last 3 months from the same period of the previous year. At least one worker is sent on paid leave (in accordance with a specific labour-management agreement).	Sales decreased by 5% or more in the last one month from the same period of the previous year. At least one worker is sent on paid leave (in accordance with a specific labour-management agreement).
Subsidy rate for absence allowance	2/3 (SMEs), 1/2 (Others).	4/5 (SMEs), 2/3 (Others). In the case of companies that have not laid off workers: 9/10 for SMEs, 3/4 for others.
Maximum amount to be paid	JPY 8 370 (2019).	JPY 15 000. (Differentiation between companies whose sales, for instance, have decreased by 30% or more on average in the last three months compared to the same period of the previous year, or companies that supported the request for reduced business hours by prefectural governors in areas where a state of emergency has been declared, and other companies)..
Procedure	Needs to submit absence/training plan in advance.	Eliminate requirement for prior submission of leave of absence/training.
Eligible recipients	Only those insured by employment insurance.	Workers who are not insured by employment insurance are also covered.
Subsidies for education and training	2/3 (SMEs), 1/2 (others). Additional amount JPY 1 200/day.	4/5 (SMEs), 2/3 (others). Additional amount JPY 2 400 (SMEs), JPY 1 800 (others) /day. Expanded the scope of education and training, including online training conducted at home as eligible for payment.
Others	–	Established a programme for workers in SMEs and workers whose working days are not set in advance and who were forced to take leave from work by employers because of the COVID-19 situation and not able to receive leave allowances.

Source: OECD Secretariat based on https://www.mhlw.go.jp/stf/seisakunitsuite/bunya/koyou_roudou/koyou/kyufukin/pageL07.html.

Due to these expansions, employment adjustment subsidies in Japan were paid out on an unprecedented scale. In 2020, the amount paid out exceeded JPY 3 trillion (about 0.6% of nominal GDP in 2020) and the number of cases paid out totalled about 3 million. These are approximately four to five times larger than in 2009, when employment adjustment subsidies were greatly expanded due to the financial crisis. The peak was reached seven months after the COVID-19 outbreak in August 2020, when around JPY 570 billion in payment decisions were made (Ministry of Health, Labour and Welfare, 2021[2]). The payment rate followed very closely the increase in cases of the virus, as the government was able to quickly react to the increases in short-term unemployment and business closures. This short processing time enabled many companies and workers to receive payments in a timely manner, mitigating some of the negative employment and income effects of the pandemic.

Figure 2.1. Employment adjustment subsidies were paid on an unprecedented scale during the COVID-19 pandemic

Number of cases and amount of payment of employment adjustment subsidy

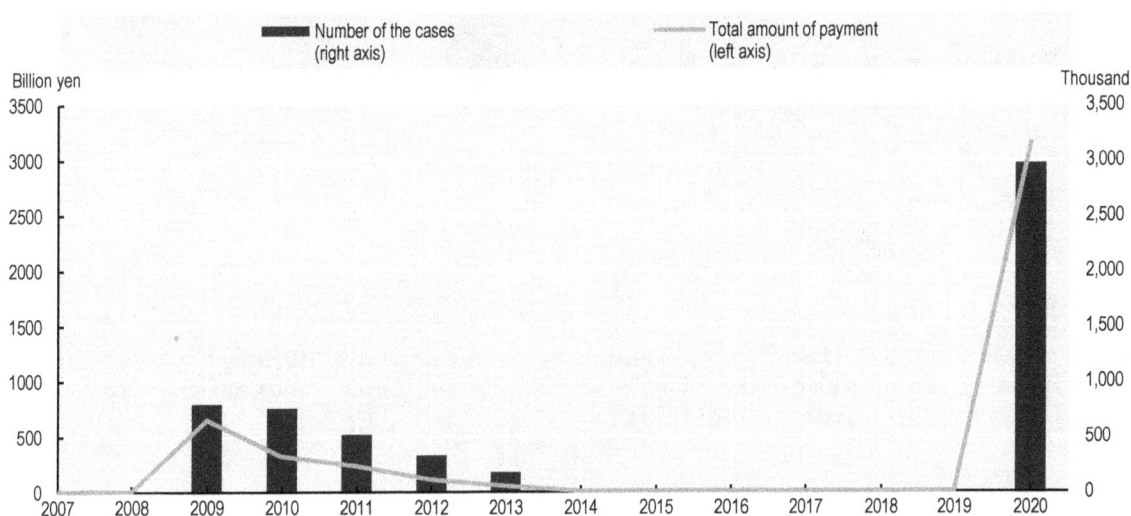

Note: Figures are in fiscal years; 2020 means from April 2020 to March 2021. Figures include payments related to education and training.
Source: The Ministry of Health, Labour and Welfare.

Many OECD countries introduced or expanded job retention schemes during the pandemic (Box 2.1), and the use of the employment adjustment subsidies was particularly important in the sectors most affected by the confinement and social distancing measures. In several countries, more than 50% of jobs in hotels and restaurants were supported by job retention schemes in the second quarter of 2020 (OECD, 2021[3]). In Japan, employment adjustment subsidies were also widely used in the food, drink and accommodation industries. According to a company survey conducted by the Japan Institute for Labour Policy and Training, 78% of firms in the food, drink and accommodation industries and 49% of firms in the manufacturing industry reported having received subsidies by September 2021 (Panel A of Figure 2.2).

While the use of subsidies in Japan was closely related to the sector of firms, firm size had little influence on take up rates (Panel B of Figure 2.2). Indeed, although 46% of middle-sized firms with 100 to 299 employees received the subsidies during the pandemic, more than one-third of firms with 1 to 99 employees and firms with 300 or more employees also received the subsidy, indicating that retention schemes reached firms regardless of their size.

The Japanese Government estimates that Japan's employment adjustment subsidies had the effect of curbing the rise in the unemployment rate by about 2-3 percentage points during 2020 (Ministry of Health, Labour and Welfare, 2021[2]; Cabinet Office, 2021[4]). Given Japan's low unemployment rate to date, this reduction is significant, even though these estimates do not take into account deadweight effects (i.e. the risk of supporting jobs that do not need support), or the possibility that support is going to jobs that have become permanently unviable.

Figure 2.2. Those industries most affected by the COVID-19 crisis benefitted the most from job retention schemes

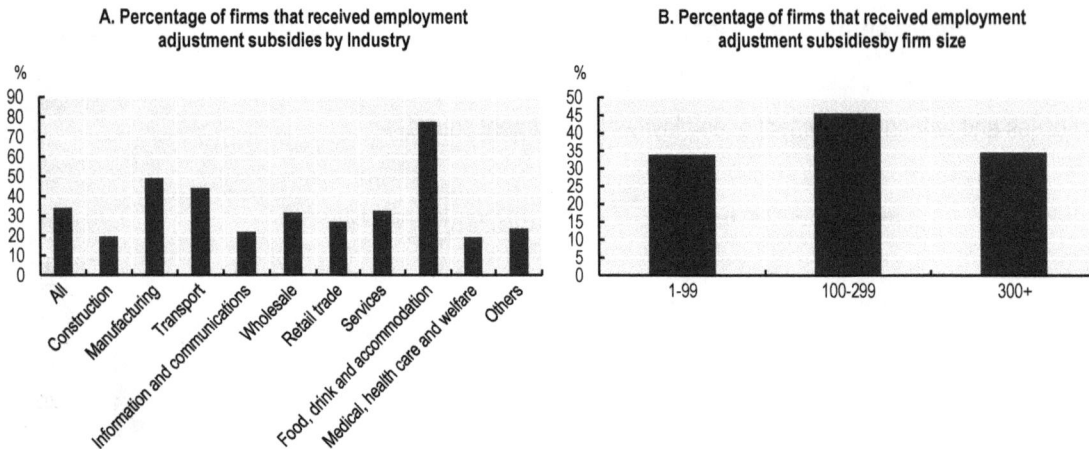

A. Percentage of firms that received employment adjustment subsidies by Industry

B. Percentage of firms that received employment adjustment subsidiesby firm size

Note: The percentage of firms reporting that they had applied for and received employment adjustment subsidies refers to September 2021.
Source: Japan Institute for Labour Policy and Training (2021), "Fifth Survey on the Impact of the New Type of Coronavirus Infection on Business Management", https://www.jil.go.jp/press/documents/20211224.pdf.

Box 2.1. Introduction and expansion of job retention schemes in other OECD countries

Japan was not the only OECD country expanding job retention schemes during the pandemic. When the COVID-19 crisis hit in the spring of 2020, nearly all OECD countries used employment retention systems to provide timely and extensive assistance to firms and workers affected by social distancing. While 16 OECD countries already had job retention schemes in place prior to COVID-19, 20 additional countries – including the United Kingdom and Australia – introduced new schemes throughout the health crisis. Preliminary estimates suggest that job retention schemes may have saved up to 21 million jobs across the OECD in the initial period of the COVID-19 crisis (OECD, 2021[3]).

Some OECD countries operating job retention schemes during the pandemic differentiated the support offered according to firm size, profitability, sector or region, with the aim of targeting those employers that were most affected by social-distancing requirements (Table 2.2). For instance, in mid-2020, Portugal adapted its scheme to provide more generous benefits for companies with greater turnover losses. Similarly, from mid-2021 in Austria, only firms in certain industries or those that suffered a drop in turnover of at least 50% between autumn 2019 and autumn 2020 received full job retention amounts. Korea also restricted its programme to firms in financial difficulties and designated 14 sectors (including transportation and tourism) as requiring special employment support due to the particularly negative impacts of the COVID-19 and seven regions as employment crisis areas. Yet, the vast majority of OECD countries (including Belgium, Chile, the Czech Republic, Denmark, Finland, Germany, Greece, Norway, the Slovak Republic, Sweden, Switzerland, and the United States) did not differentiate their support (OECD, 2022[5]).

Table 2.2. OECD countries that targeted job retention scheme to firms and workers most affected by COVID-19 restrictions

Situation as of November 2021

	By firm size	By firm profitability	By sector	By region
Japan	•			•
Austria	•		•	
Colombia	•			
France		•	•	•
Italy	•		•	
Korea	•	•	•	•
Luxembourg			•	
Netherlands		•		
Portugal		•		
Spain	•			

Note: OECD countries that had a job retention scheme in place in November 2021 but did not differentiate support by firm size, firm profitability, sector or region: Belgium, Chile, the Czech Republic, Denmark, Finland, Germany, Greece, Norway, the Slovak Republic, Sweden, Switzerland, and the United States.
Source: OECD Questionnaire on Policy Responses to the COVID-19 Crisis.

2.1.2. A shift from employment retention to upskilling and reskilling policies is required

During 2021, many countries scaled back their employment retention schemes, and by November 2021 13 of the 20 OECD countries that had implemented special COVID-19 retention schemes had terminated these schemes (Panel A of Figure 2.3). At their peak use in April/May 2020, job retention schemes were used by an average of 20% of employed people in selected OECD countries (where data on take-up rate are available), but the use had declined to 1% by November/December 2021 (OECD, 2022[6]). The substantial decline in utilisation reflects to some extent both the resumption of economic activity due to an easing in social-distancing requirements and widespread vaccination, and the accompanying phasing out of job retention schemes.

Since the number of workers who received the employment adjustment subsidy is not publicly available in Japan, it is difficult to compare the use of such subsidies with other countries. However, OECD estimates based on a 2020 sample survey by the Ministry of Health, Labour and Welfare on companies receiving employment adjustment subsidies suggest that about 3% of workers used the scheme from April to October. This proportion is small compared to other OECD countries. In comparison, 65% of workers in New Zealand received subsidies in 2020. On the other hand, unlike in other OECD countries, Japan's use of employment adjustment subsidies did not slow down in 2021 and has remained relatively stable since the beginning of the crisis. Indeed, the number of applications for the subsidies in Japan increased sharply after May 2020, peaking in August to October, and continued to remain high even as the number of infected persons declined in 2021, with an average of about 64 000 applications per week (Figure 2.3). This may be partly due to the relatively long duration of emergency and confinement measures compared with other countries, with their implementation throughout 2021.

Figure 2.3. The use of job retention schemes has declined sharply in many OECD countries but has remained nearly the same level in Japan

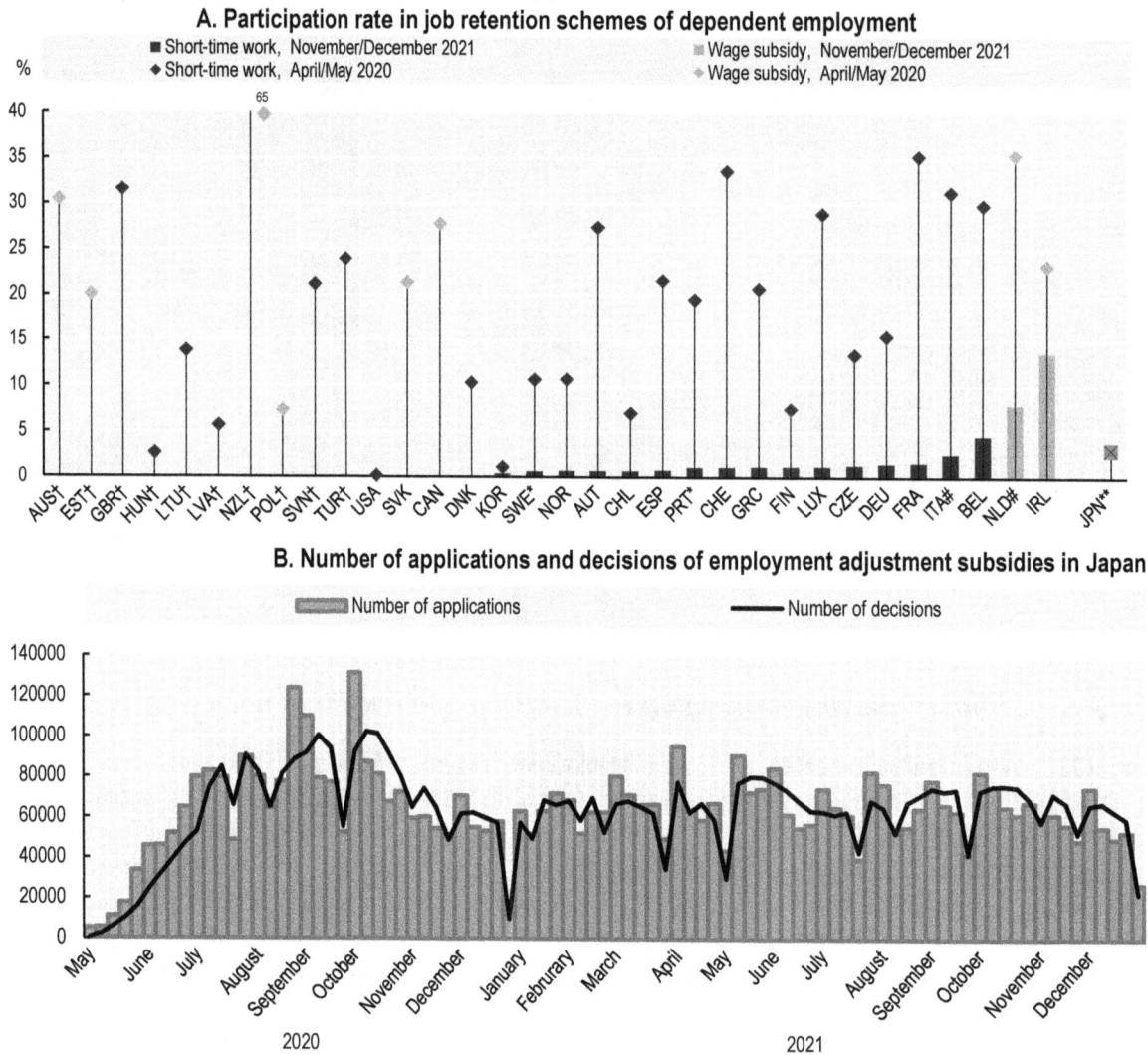

A. Participation rate in job retention schemes of dependent employment

B. Number of applications and decisions of employment adjustment subsidies in Japan

Note: A. Take-up rates are calculated as a percentage of all dependent employees in Q1 2020. † Australia, Estonia, Hungary, Latvia, Lithuania, New Zealand, Poland, Slovenia, United Kingdom and Turkey: Scheme no longer operational or not widely available. *Latest data refer to October 2021 (Czech Republic and Luxembourg), August 2021 (Portugal) and September 2021 (Sweden). #The Netherlands: Estimates based on the total use during the reference period and the assumption that support is provided for no more than three months during this period. #Italy: Data estimated based on the number of authorised hours. The United States: Data refer to short-time compensation benefits. No information on take-up available for Colombia, Iceland and Israel. No scheme present in Costa Rica and Mexico. B. Numbers are weekly counts. **Japan: Average monthly number of employees who received employment adjustment subsidies including Emergency Employment Stabilization Subsidy from April to October 2020, which is estimated using the information about the amount of employment adjustment subsidies and actual payments in the sample survey conducted by the Ministry of Health, Labour and Welfare, divided by the average number of employees during the same period.

Source: National sources; OECD (2022[5]), *OECD Employment Outlook 2022: Building Back More Inclusive Labour Markets*, https://doi.org/10.1787/1bb305a6-en; Ministry of Health, Labour and Welfare (2021[2]), 2021 Labour Economics Analysis, https://www.mhlw.go.jp/wp/hakusyo/roudou/20/dl/20-2.pdf; Japanese Labour Force Survey; OECD calculation based on payments of employment adjustment subsidies published by the Ministry of Health, Labour and Welfare (https://www.mhlw.go.jp/stf/seisakunitsuite/bunya/koyou_roudou/koyou/kyufukin/pageL07.html).

Maintaining a stable employment rate during the pandemic has been a policy concern of the Japanese Government, but it has come at a cost. As of the end of March 2022, the government had approved over 6 million applications (the cumulative total number of firms making applications) for employment adjustment subsidies (Ministry of Health, Labour and Welfare, 2022[7]). These have helped mitigate several of the negative labour market consequences experienced in other OECD countries during the pandemic, and helped maintain a stable employment rate. However, the unprecedented expenditure on employment adjustment subsidies has also had significant financial implications. Various employment measures, including employment adjustment subsidies, are traditionally financed by employment insurance. Due to the increase in the provision of employment adjustment subsidies, etc. because of COVID-19, the cost could not be covered by insurance premium revenues and the government responded by drawing on its reserve fund for employment measures, which was over JPY 1.5 trillion in 2019, and which dropped to zero in 2020 (Figure 2.4). In order to maintain the provision of employment adjustment subsidies, etc., the government drew on the reserve fund for unemployment benefits and the financial situation of employment insurance has deteriorated. The insurance premium rate was lowered from 2017, but it became necessary to raise the insurance premium rate due to the deterioration of the insurance finances. However, considering that the economic situation was in the process of recovery and that it was necessary to implement the measure to reduce the insurance premium burden, the premium rate did not return to the rate originally stipulated by the law (1.55%) and the law was amended to raise the premium rate for employment insurance to 0.95% (from April 2022) and to 1.35% (from October 2022). Considering the stable unemployment rate in Japan, it would be worth considering phasing out special measures for employment adjustment subsidies gradually, taking into account the situation in the sectors most affected by the COVID-19 pandemic, and shift the focus towards policies to support labour mobility, such as upskilling and reskilling workers, and subsidising labour mobility from downsized firms to growing industries.

Figure 2.4. In response to COVID-19, the government consumed a large portion of the unemployment insurance reserve

Change in reserve for employment insurance

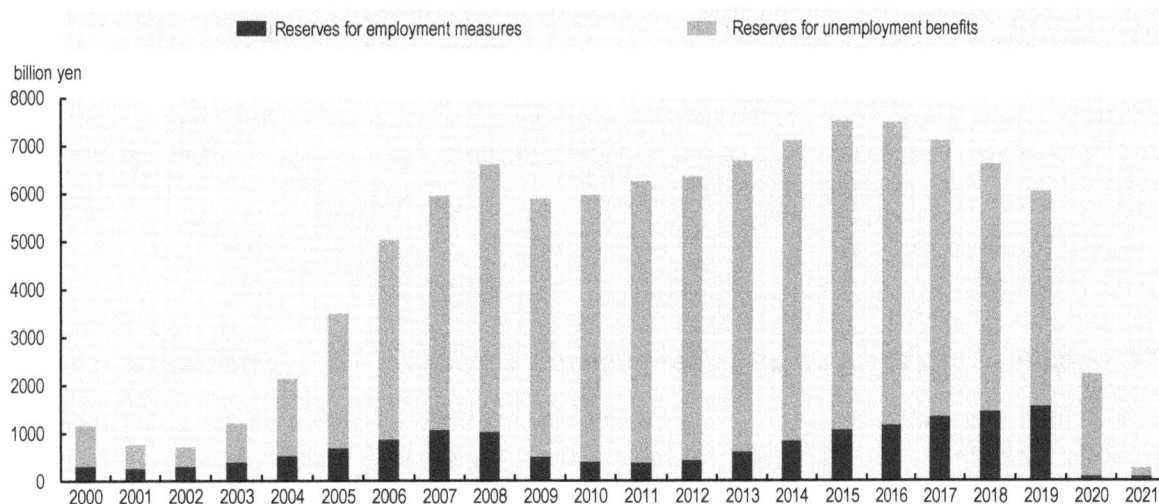

Source: OECD analysis based on Ministry of Health, Labour and Welfare data.

Fears that employment subsidies may have undesirable consequences on the hiring of graduates seem unfounded for the time being. In the 1990s and early 2000s, efforts to maintain high employment levels despite prolonged economic contractions resulted in what became known as the "Employment ice age", which had a negative effect on the hiring of new graduates in Japan (Ohta, S., Y. Genda and A. Kondo, 2008[8]). During the period, many new graduates faced challenges in obtaining stable employment and those cohorts are still facing less stable employment than older and younger generations. It remains to be seen if such trends resurface after the COVID-19 pandemic (OECD, 2021[9]). According to the "Survey of Employment Situation of University Graduates in March 2022" conducted by the Ministry of Education, Culture, Sports, Science and Technology and the Ministry of Health, Labour and Welfare, the employment rate for those who graduated from university in March 2022 is 96%. While this is slightly lower than the most recent peak of 98% in 2018, it is still 5 percentage points higher than the one experienced by graduates during the employment ice age and the global financial crisis (around 91%).

A priority going forward is to learn from the experience of the COVID-19 crisis and assess the effectiveness of job retention scheme in saving jobs and supporting job creation. In addition to the particular concern about the deadweight effect that job retention schemes can have in supporting jobs that do not require subsidy support (OECD, 2020[10]), potential concerns have arisen about the displacement effect, i.e. the potential for the support to go toward jobs that have become permanently unviable. Keeping workers in non-viable jobs not only increases the financial costs of job retention scheme, but may also impede recovery by delaying reallocation from low to high productivity firms. Further, employers can get stuck in working for companies that do not have the capacity to invest in their workforce, and their skills can become obsolete much faster. Key to such an assessment should be an analysis of the effectiveness of employment retention systems in protecting different types of workers from the risk of unemployment and in supporting longer-term career paths. For instance, the OECD has so far conducted such a country evaluation for Switzerland, and several countries, including France and Sweden, have already evaluated their programmes or are planning to do so over 2022-24 (OECD, 2022[5]).

As mentioned above, Japan's employment adjustment subsidies also cover the cost of education and training and this can be seen as an investment: training during absences can improve workers' current job-related skills and re-employment prospects. For this reason, education and training will continue to be an important component of job retention schemes, even after the pandemic. However, it is difficult to analyse the effectiveness of these subsidies in Japan, because of limited data collection. When looking at other countries that introduced financial incentives to promote participation in training while on reduced working time, participation in training during short-time work was about 20% in France and close to 30% in Spain (OECD, 2022[6]). In order to evaluate the effectiveness of each subsidy programme, it would be important to establish a mechanism to collect disaggregated data, such as data on the characteristics of workers who received subsidies by subsidies type.

2.2. Digitalisation of career guidance services during the pandemic

2.2.1. Despite policy attention on career guidance services, its use remains low in Japan

With the COVID-19 pandemic, career guidance has become more prominent on the policy agenda of several OECD countries. Career guidance can be used as a policy lever to facilitate employment transitions and identify appropriate up-skilling and re-skilling opportunities. Throughout the pandemic, many adults had to transition to different occupations and sectors, and therefore had an increasing need for assistance in identifying sustainable employment and relevant training. As social distancing measures prompted the rapid digitalisation of career guidance services, governments have quickly realised that digitalisation allows for more flexibility in how and when career guidance is delivered, which helps to overcome a lack of time as a key barrier to accessing career guidance (OECD, 2021[11]). The digitalisation of career guidance made the service more accessible to jobseekers and workers during lockdown periods, although it required large-scale advertisement to raise awareness of the services.

Similarly to other OECD countries, Japanese authorities have encouraged the expansion of career guidance in recent years, and have promoted existing services such as the "Self-Career Dock system" (OECD, 2021[12]). In 2020, the government established several support centres for career development and set up a system to provide free online or in-person career counselling sessions. Yet, the participation rate of career guidance among Japanese workers remains low compared with other countries. According to the 2020 Basic Survey on Human Resource Development, while 38% of Japanese companies offer career guidance services, the percentage of workers who used career guidance over the 12 months between April 2019 and May 2020 was less than 10% (Figure 2.5). According to the OECD 2020 Survey of Career Guidance for Adults (SCGA), usage rates were much higher in other countries – for instance in Germany (29%), France (30%), and Australia (49%).

Figure 2.5. The use of career guidance services by Japanese workers remains low

Percentage of workers who used career guidance in the past 12 months, 2020

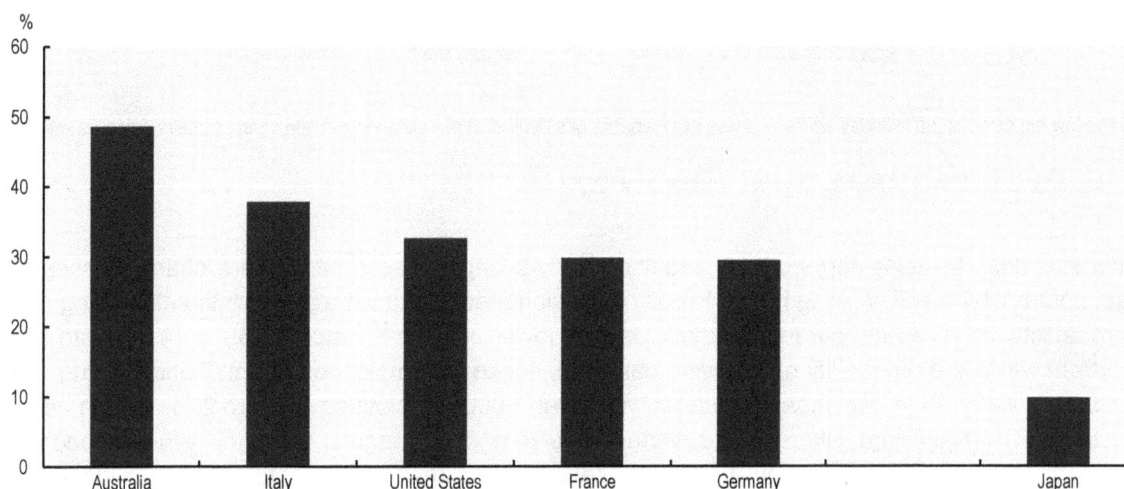

Note: In Japan, the target population is workers in companies with 30 or more employees; in Australia, France, Germany, Italy, and the United States, the target population is workers in companies with 10 or more employees. The percentage of respondents in Japan refers to those who received career consulting during fiscal year 2019; for the other countries, the percentage of respondent's refers to those who spoke with a career guidance advisor in the past 12 months at the time of the survey, i.e. 2020 for Italy, United States, France and Germany, and 2021 for Australia.
Source: OECD 2020 Survey of Career Guidance for Adults (SCGA); Japanese Basic Survey of Human Resource Development (2020).

Like in other countries, there are large differences in the use of career guidance services in Japan depending on the workers' socio-economic characteristics (Figure 2.6). For example, while almost one in every five workers aged 20-29 receive career guidance, this proportion drops to 6% for those aged 50-59. The likelihood of using career guidance services also increases with firm size, and for full-time employees relative to part-time employees. Further, there are significant differences by industry, with relatively high participation rates in industries with larger shares of high-skilled workers, such as the information and communication sector and the financial and professional/technical services industries, and significantly lower rates in industries that employ more low-skilled workers such as wholesale/retail and accommodation/restaurant services. Inequality in the use of career guidance is of concern, as it indicates that the services are not reaching groups that could benefit from it the most, namely workers in SMEs and non-regular workers.

Figure 2.6. Percentage of career consulting services received varies by socio-economic characteristics

Percentage of adult who used career consulting service in the past 12 months by socio-economic characteristics, 2020

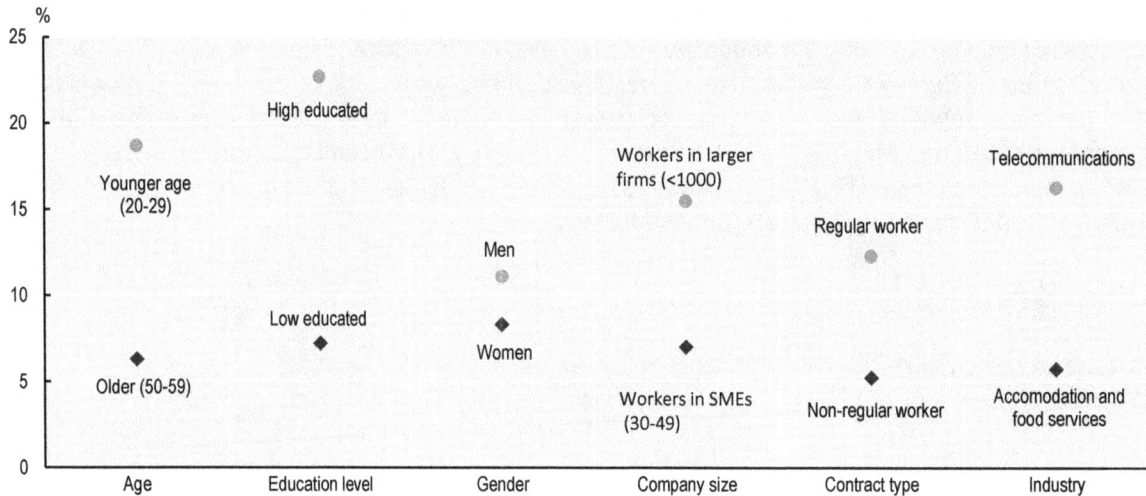

Notes: The low educated group includes adults with less than a bachelor's degree. High educated indicates only bachelor's degree with liberal arts.
Source: Japanese Basic Survey of Human Resource Development (2020).

Econometric analysis helps corroborate these findings by taking into account workers' characteristics such as age, contract type and working hours. Probit regression results show that, everything else being equal, the probability of receiving career guidance is 7% lower for those aged 50-59 compared to those aged 20-29, while the probability of receiving career guidance for employees of small and medium-sized firms is 6% lower than for those in firms with over 1 000 employees (Figure 2.7). Japan is also characterised by significant differences between regular and non-regular workers. While econometric analysis for Chile, France, Germany, Italy, New Zealand, and the United States does not identify any significant effect of workers' contract type on the use of career guidance (OECD, 2021[11]), in Japan the probability of using of career guidance for non-regular workers is 3% lower than that for regular workers. This may reflect the greater difference in attitudes toward careers between regular and non-regular workers in Japan compared with other OECD countries.

Figure 2.7 also shows no significant difference in the probability of receiving career counselling by education level or working hours. This suggests that education and lack of time due to long working hours are not the biggest barriers to career guidance. An important caveat is that the regression analysis does not capture lack of time due to personal responsibilities – e.g. child caring – and there tends to be a positive correlation between personal responsibilities and working part-time.

In addition, the probability of receiving career guidance was 5% higher for workers in firms that had an internal career counselling system than for workers in firms that did not. This underscores the need for government support to increase the number of companies that actively provide career-related consultations, including the Self-Career Dock system.

Figure 2.7. Effects of career guidance services by socio-economic and demographic characteristics

Average marginal effects from a probit regression

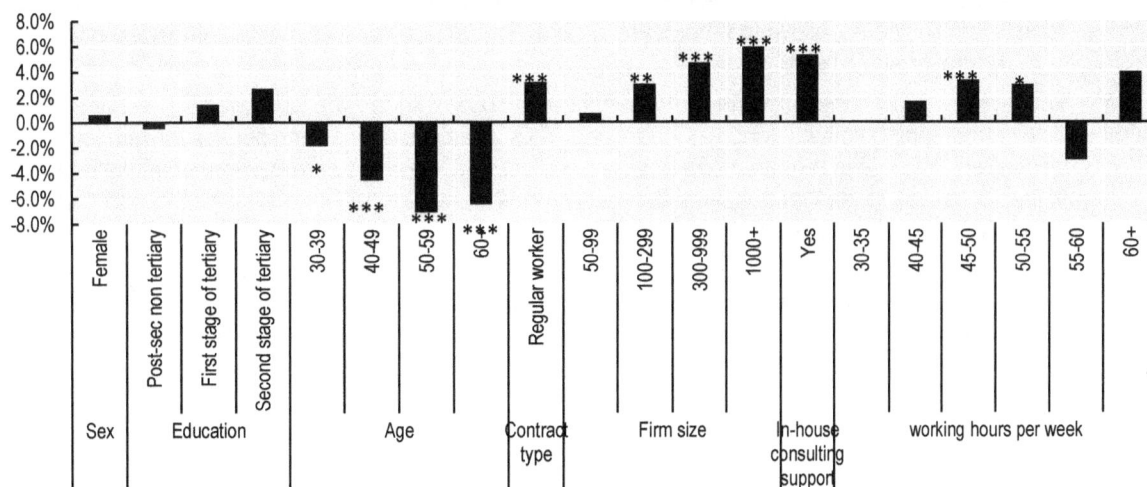

Note: ***, statistically significant at the 1% level, **, statistically significant at the 5% level and *, statistically significant at the 10% level. The figure shows estimates of the average marginal impact of selected variables on receiving career guidance services. The benchmark group has the following characteristics: male (sex), upper secondary education or below (education), aged 20-29 (age), non-regular worker (contract type), 30-49 (firm size), firms that do not provide in-house career consulting support, 35-40 hours (working hours per week). These effects are estimated with controls for industry, occupation, job title, turnover rate, and the share of non-regular workers in a firm.
Source: OECD analysis based on Japanese Basic Survey of Human Resource Development (2020) supported by the Ministry of Health, Labour and Welfare.

2.2.2. The COVID-19 pandemic has fostered the digitisation of career guidance

The restrictions on interpersonal contacts caused by the pandemic have reiterated the importance of an efficient digitalisation of administrative systems. One of the major impacts of the COVID-19 crisis was indeed to prompt changes in the way public services are delivered, accelerating the digitisation and organisational reforms currently underway in Japan. On the employment side in particular, there has been a shift toward providing online services to obtain employment adjustment subsidies and career assistance in the public employment services (PES) (Table 2.3).

> **Box 2.2. Timeline of digitalisation of career guidance services in Japan**
>
> - August 2020: the government released a website to submit online applications for employment adjustment subsidies, allowing employers to apply for the subsidies at any time from a computer at work, home, or elsewhere.
> - September 2020: the government launched a pilot virtual job counselling service using videoconferencing software such as Zoom, etc. This virtual job counselling service targets registered jobseekers who live in remote areas or who have difficulty coming to the PES for consultations. The online consultation services include advice on how to write CVs, interview preparation and job referrals. They will be extended to major PES offices across Japan in 2022.
> - September 2021: Job placement services provided online. Jobseekers can now log into the PES website and apply for vacancies online. They can also view their history of job applications and the results of acceptance or rejection. Such direct application to vacancies is beneficial for both employers and workers: in fact, it has the advantage that jobseekers can now apply for jobs directly without having to go through the PES, while companies receive more applications.

Table 2.3. The PES in Japan has facilitated online service in a variety of areas

Policy Contents	Start of the scheme	Short description	Results
Online application for employment adjustment subsidies	August 2020	Possibility to apply for employment adjustment subsidies online without the need to go to the Public Employment Security Office	About 5% of all applications for employment adjustment subsidies have been sent online
Online career guidance consultations	September 2020	Launched a pilot virtual job counselling service through videoconferencing without having to visit the Public Employment Security Office	Number of PES providing online job consultation: 261 nationwide, 48% of the total PES (as of the end of December 2021) Number of online job consultations: 8 678 (from April 2021 to December 2021)
Online job placement	September 2021	Jobseekers can make online job applications and get online job placement through the website of the Public Employment Security Office	Number of online registrations: 4 911 (number of new job applications in December 2021) Number of cases in which online job placement resulted in employment: 51 (December 2021)

Source: OECD Questionnaire on Policy Responses to the COVID-19 crisis.

Since their establishment in April 2020, the Career Development Support centres have offered online services to jobseekers and other interested adults, and the COVID-19 pandemic has accelerated the diffusion of remote career guidance throughout Japan.[2] A survey conducted by the Japan Institute for Labour Policy and Training in November 2020 (hereinafter referred to as Japanese Online Career Guidance Survey) found that around one-third of those who had received career guidance in the past had experienced online consultation, and of those, about half experienced online career guidance after the COVID-19 outbreak, suggesting that the efforts by the Japanese Government in facilitating online services have had an effect (The Japan Institute for Labor Policy Training, 2022[13]). The move to online career guidance has not been limited to public institutions and the progression in online provision has continued. According to a nation-wide survey of career counsellors, including those in the private sector, the percentage of career consultants who provide online career guidance increased from 53% in 2020 to 65% in 2021, showing that the trend towards more digital services since the COVID-19 outbreak has continued (Japan Manpower, 2021[14]). Overall, the move towards online guidance services in Japan is parallel to what happened in other OECD countries during the crisis (see Box 2.3 for more information about other OECD experiences).

Box 2.3. The move towards online guidance services across the OECD

During the pandemic, the need for social distancing made it impossible to carry out on-site services and career guidance providers had to shift delivery towards fully remote alternatives. The percentage of respondents to the 2020 Inter-Agency Working Group on Work-Based Learning (IAG-WBL)'s Career Guidance Survey who report providing fully remote career guidance services jumped from 6% in the pre-pandemic period to almost 80% during the pandemic (OECD, 2022[15]).

In particular, several OECD countries have improved access to career guidance by creating online portals. For example, adults in Greece can now have a real time conversation with a career guidance advisor through the EOPPEP Internet Portal for Adults. In Canada, a COVID-19 resource page was launched on the Job Bank website in mid-April 2020. In the United States, information on how to file for unemployment and on other benefits available for recently unemployed workers had been made available through the *CareerOneStop* portal (OECD, 2021[11]). In Belgium, the Flemish public employment service launched the online platform *Mijn loopbaan* (My career), where visitors can view their work experience, how much they earned and how much pension they have built up. Users can create a fully personalised online portfolio (keeping track of competences and qualifications), create a CV and upload it to an online platform used by employers (Cedefop, European Commission, ETF, ILO, OECD, UNESCO, 2021[16]).

In addition to creating online portals for career guidance, during the crisis other OECD countries have provided specific support to help counsellors adapt their services to remote delivery. For example, France made particular efforts to ensure that all career guidance advisors could telework by equipping them with laptops and mobile phones (Cedefop, 2020[17]). Ireland provided counsellors with training to share good practices on delivery of guidance online during COVID-19 (Department of Education and Skills, 2020[18]).

Table 2.4. Changes to online career guidance portals during the COVID-19 pandemic

Country	Changes made or planned
Australia	• Strong focus on connecting people with information about current labour market changes, government support during the pandemic and study options such as short courses that will equip individuals to re-enter the workforce as soon as possible.
Belgium	• More online services
Canada	A COVID-19 resource page was launched in mid-April, on the Job Bank website (www.jobbank.gc.ca). It has become a popular destination for users to find information related to work during COVID-19.
Czech Republic	• A chat bot has been launched on the *MoLSA* portal, which helps visitors answer basic questions.
Denmark	• National response to strengthen career guidance for adults being unemployed due to COVID-19.
Estonia	• Special subsection describing online career services was added to the online portal
France	• Any change affecting the rights and/or the way in which they can be exercised will be indicated on the portal 'Mon conseil en évolution professionnelle'.
Greece	• The EOPPEP Internet Portal for Adults will provide to the visitor the opportunity for receiving distant counselling services, to have a real time direct conversation with a career guidance counsellor through a special form that will be filled by the visitor.
Ireland	• *Careersportal* provided links to various national agencies and guidelines.
Korea	• Process to strengthen mobile access is underway.
Spain	• The portal www.sepe.es reinforced its virtual tools for career guidance.
Sweden	• No specific career guidance services were developed specifically to meet the COVID-19 situation, but the intensification and prioritisation of digital career guidance are increasing.

Source: OECD 2020 Policy Questionnaire 'Career Guidance for Adults'.

2.2.3. Need to further promote the use of digital tools to benefit all

In Japan, those who have experienced online career guidance generally tend to rate it highly: about 60% of respondents to the Japanese online career guidance survey considered that online career guidance is useful, compared to only 50% of respondents who answered that in-person career guidance is useful (The Japan Institute for Labor Policy Training, 2022[13]). Online career guidance has the advantage of not being tied to a specific time and place, and encourages users to be more candid. Indeed, many survey respondents argued that online career guidance was useful because they could receive it at a convenient time (57%), because it is easy to talk frankly with career consultants as the process seems less daunting (32%), and because respondents could consult at a convenient location, regardless of where they live (31%).

On the other hand, international experience shows that vulnerable groups facing poorer labour outcomes often had difficulty accessing digital devices and did not have the necessary skills to benefit from digital services (Cedefop, European Commission, ETF, ILO, OECD, UNESCO, 2021[16]). The Survey of Adult Skills (PIAAC) shows that while Japan has a higher share of digital problem solvers (42%) than the OECD adult average (32%), it also has a higher proportion of adults without basic ICT skills (25% vs. 19%) (OECD, 2021[12]). This suggests that, similarly to the situation observed in other countries, also in Japan certain vulnerable groups may not be receiving the necessary support.

Looking at the characteristics of people receiving online career guidance, 67% of those who live in large urban areas have taken online career guidance, compared to 45% of those who lived in rural and suburban areas. In addition, while 69% of those with online learning experience prior to the outbreak of COVID-19 had experienced online career guidance, only 39% of those who first experienced online learning after the onset of COVID-19 had online career guidance (The Japan Institute for Labor Policy Training, 2022[13]). These results show that those who do not live in urban areas and those who are not familiar with online learning may be less likely to access online career guidance.

In addition, when looking at differences in preferences for consultation methods by demographic characteristics, people with high levels of education (university graduates), in managerial, professional, or clerical occupations, and working for large companies reported a relatively higher preference for online career guidance, while women, the low educated, those with lower incomes (annual income below JPY 4 million), those in sales, service, or production process occupations, and workers in small and medium-sized companies reported a greater preference for telephone or email (Figure 2.8). These results suggest that those in precarious occupations either do not have access to stable internet or a device at home that would allow for online consultation, and/or do not have enough digital skills. A third option is that, due to the generally low digitalisation of services in Japan, underrepresented adults are not as used to navigating digital services as their more privileged counterparts, and therefore do not have the culture or confidence in using digital services.

Taking ownership of own career development also affects preferences in delivery methods. In the Japanese online career guidance survey, those who answered "I want to plan my career by myself" 26% said that online career guidance at home was the preferred medium, and 30% said that telephone or e-mail was the preferred medium. For those who answered "I want the company to develop my career plan" only 14% said that online career guidance at home was the preferred medium, while 47% said that telephone or e-mail was the preferred medium (The Japan Institute for Labor Policy Training, 2022[13]). This might reflect a correlation between education, career planning ownership and confidence. Those who are more educated and better equipped to make decisions and formulate plans about their career, are more confident to present and discuss them digitally "face-to-face". On the other hand, those with less education may be happier to leave the career planning to their employer as they know less about their options, and therefore prefer phone delivery where it is easier to be less involved in the guidance session.

Remote career guidance services are likely to continue after the pandemic. The availability of digital devices and the development of digital skills are important to enable access, but well-designed outreach efforts are also needed to ensure equity of access. The government has continued to promote the use of digital tools and online provision of career guidance, while at the same time ensuring that demographic groups that already underutilise these services are not further alienated by the digital transition.

Figure 2.8. Only certain groups of adults opted for an online delivery of career guidance services

Career guidance preference by workers' characteristics

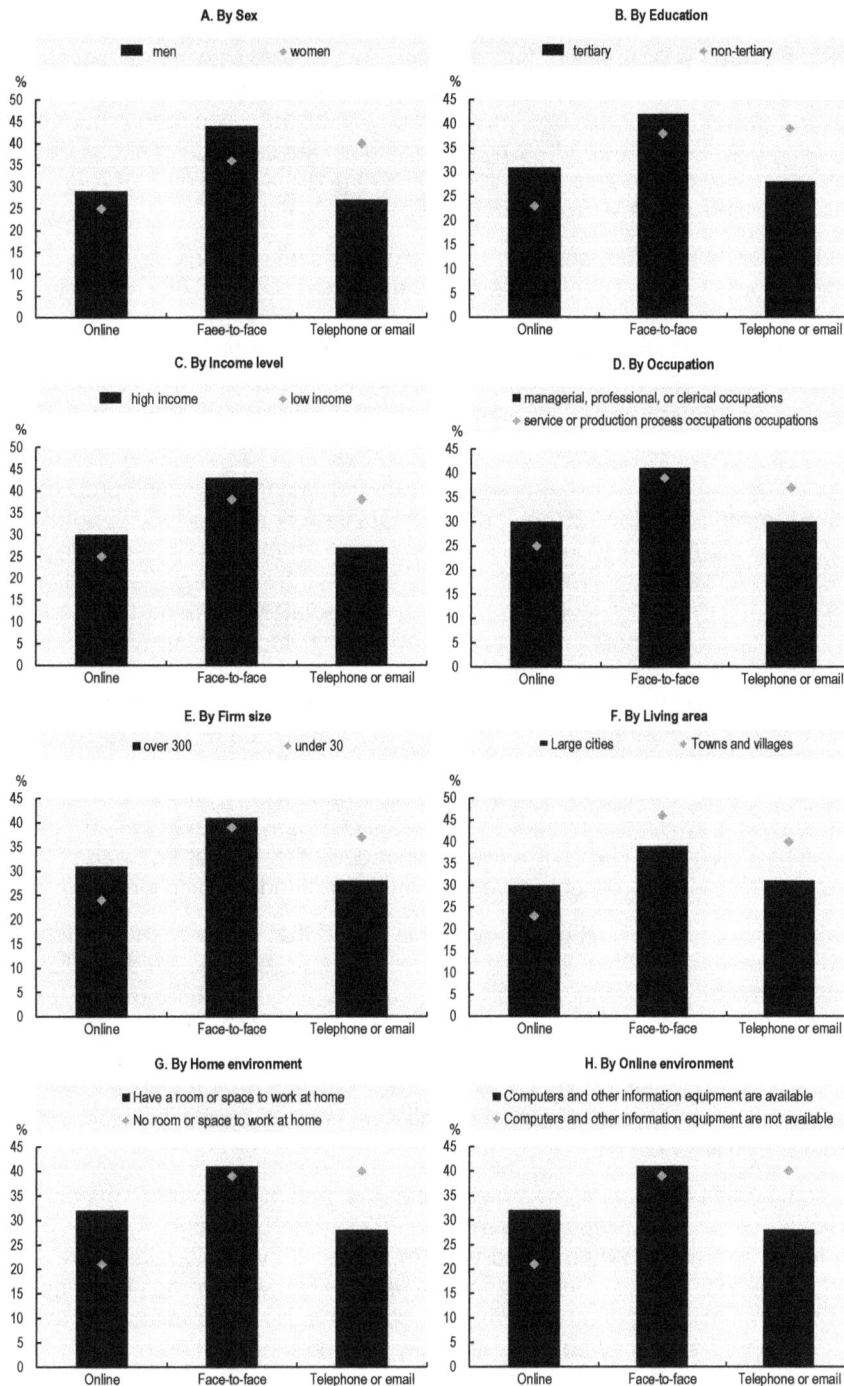

Note: Online includes both at home and outside of home.
Source: Japan Institute for Labour Policy and Training (2022), "Research on career-related qualifications and online career support in developed countries" https://www.jil.go.jp/institute/siryo/2022/documents/0250.pdf.

2.3. The implementation of new teleworking practices

2.3.1. If implemented correctly, there can be a positive link between teleworking and productivity

The COVID-19 crisis provided a large-scale natural experiment to assess how semi-compulsory teleworking practices served as an effective means for maintaining firms' productivity and enhancing workers' well-being. Previous studies have shown that telework can improve work-life balance and reduce commuting time, while at the same time improving corporate performance by increasing worker satisfaction and labour efficiency through more focused work and fewer distractions (Godart, O., H. Görg and A. Hanley, 2017[19]; Beckmann, 2016[20]; Beckmann, M., T. Cornelissen and M. Kräkel, 2017[21]; Monteiro, 2019[22]).

Telework can also improve firm performance by facilitating cost savings. Indeed, it can directly lower capital costs by reducing the amount of office space and equipment needed by firms (Bloom, N. et al., 2015[23]). Labour costs can be reduced because teleworking expands the pool of workers from which firms can recruit, thereby increasing the supply of skills and improving the match between workers and vacancies by, for example, hiring highly skilled workers who are tied to a particular location for personal reasons (Clancy, 2020[24]). In addition, employment costs may decrease if voluntary resignations and turnover decrease due to increased worker satisfaction.

However, a few studies also pointed at certain negative externalities of teleworking practices for both workers and employers. For example, Morikawa (2021[25]) shows that telework may reduce performance, noting that in the early stages of the pandemic, the productivity of teleworking employees in Japan declined by more than 30% (at the same time, however, the research concluded that the average teleworking productivity has improved by more than 10 percentage points in the year immediately following the start of the pandemic). Teleworking may also reduce labour efficiency by reducing face-to-face interactions and impairing communication, knowledge flow, and managerial oversight. Several previous studies support the notion that in-person meetings are more effective than remote communication such as email, chat, and phone calls (Bohns, 2017[26]; Roghanizad, M. and V. Bohns, 2017[27]; Battiston, D., J. Blanes and T. Kirchmaier, 2017[28]; Bonet, R. and F. Salvadora, 2017[29]). In addition to the impact on the company internally, infrequent personal communication can also have a negative impact on the company's relationships with key stakeholders, e.g. customers and suppliers, which can negatively affect the company's overall performance (Hovhannisyan, N. and W. Keller, 2019[30]). Lack of interaction may also reduce the flow of knowledge among employees, thereby reducing opportunities to acquire collective knowledge and undermining long-term productivity gains.

Overall, for telework to increase firm-level productivity, it is crucial that workers' satisfaction increases enough to offset the potential negative effects that it may also entail. Workers' satisfaction and efficiency may increase when the frequency of remote work remains relatively moderate, but may suffer due to "excessive" telework, because of the sense of loneliness and a lack of separation between personal and professional life. In other words, there is an inverse U-shaped relationship between the amount of telework and workers' efficiency, although the relationship is expected to vary by industry and occupation (OECD, 2020[31]). Teleworking also needs to be organised in a way that its potential negative effects on communication, knowledge flow, and managerial oversight are minimised.

It is also important to note that teleworking was highly effective in controlling infections during the pandemic's spread. An online survey conducted in Japan in early June 2021 indicates that nearly 27% of COVID-19 positive people contracted the virus at work. When asked what measures they would take to prevent viral infections, more than half (52%) selected "remain in-house as much as possible" with women being especially likely to do so. Moreover, preliminary findings gathered during the pandemic in Japan indicate that 56% of managers perceived telework as better than expected, stressing how the public opinion around remote work practices is also changing (Ozimek, 2020[32]).

2.3.2. Japan's push towards teleworking during the pandemic

The potential for telework in Japan is close to the OECD average. Based on studies conducted in the United States (Dingel, J. and B. Neiman, 2020[33]) and Japan (Kotera, 2020[34]), an international comparison of the feasibility of remote work by region shows that one-third of jobs in Japan are amenable to teleworking (with the maximum being 43% in Tokyo and the minimum being 24% in Aomori Prefecture) and this is comparable to the average across the OECD (Panel A of Figure 2.9). Despite this, Japan ranks relatively low in comparison to most OECD countries in terms of share of tertiary educated workers whose jobs are compatible with teleworking. An analysis based on PIAAC shows that, while Japan has a smaller difference in teleworking feasibility by education level than other OECD countries, the teleworking feasibility of tertiary educated workers is around 8 percentage points lower than the OECD average (Panel B of Figure 2.9). This may reflect Japan's occupational composition, where highly qualified individuals are more likely to work in jobs that are relatively difficult to perform through telework.

Figure 2.9. Japan's potential for telework implementation is close to the OECD average

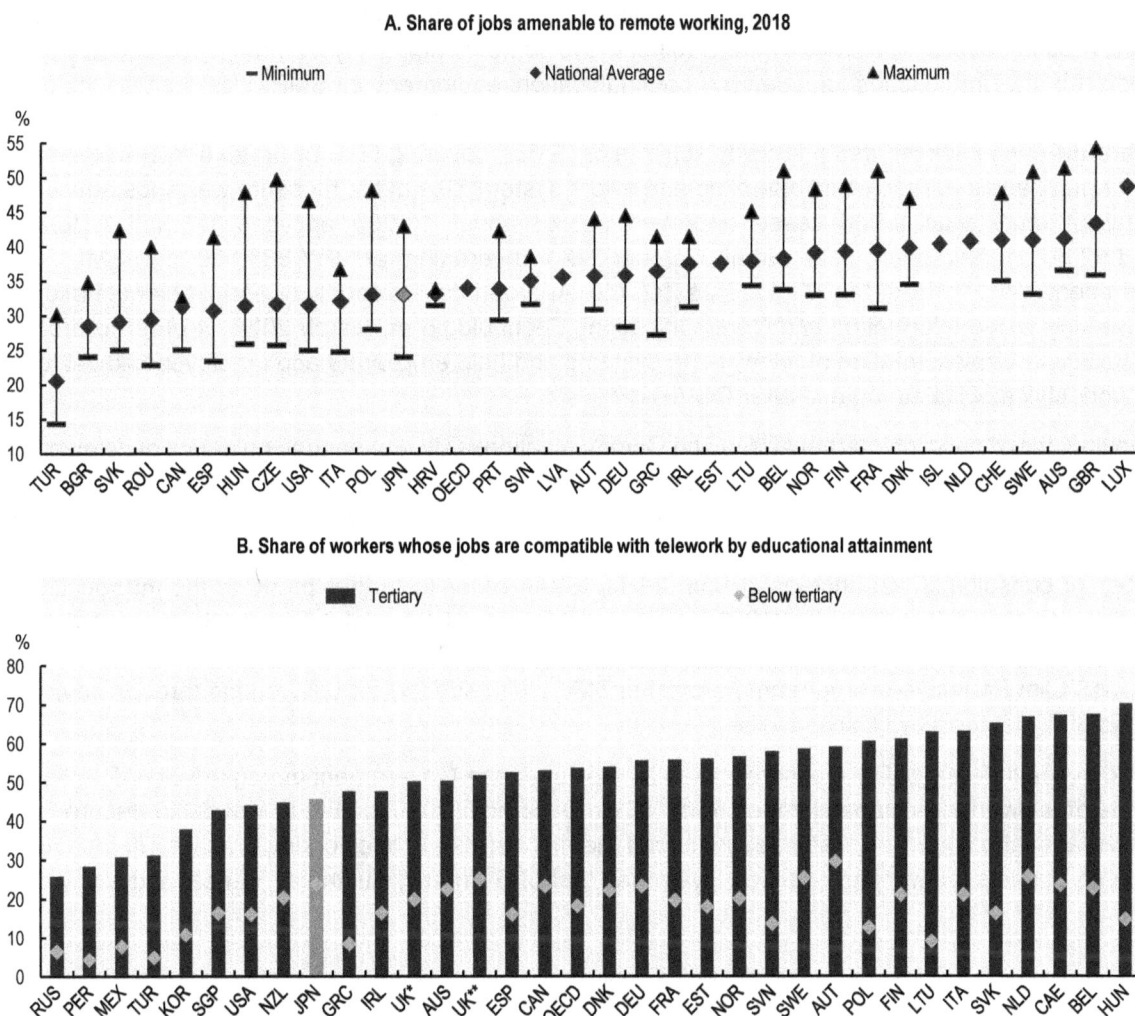

A. Share of jobs amenable to remote working, 2018

B. Share of workers whose jobs are compatible with telework by educational attainment

Note: A: Potential for remote working: The assessment of regions' capacity to adapt to remote working is based on the diversity of tasks performed in different types of occupations. For further information: OECD (2020), *Capacity for remote working can affect shutdowns' costs differently across places, OECD Policy* Note (http://www.oecd.org/coronavirus/policy-responses/capacity-for-remote-working-can-affect-lockdown-costs-differently-across-places-0e85740e/). Figures for Japan are based on Kotera (2020[34]) and the OECD average does not include Japan's data. From the perspective of estimating the upper limit of teleworking possibility of Japan, the figures are calculated by multiplying the score of whether or not teleworking is possible by the adjusted value (1-N÷3). (N is the number of items in each occupational category for which the criterion for making teleworking difficult applies in each occupational category.) B: UK* indicates Northern Ireland and UK** indicates England.

Source: OECD calculations based on American Community Survey (ACS), Australian Labour Force Survey, Canadian Labour Force Survey, European Labour Force Survey, Turkish Household Labour Force Survey, Turkish Statistical Institute and Occupational Information Network data. Data for Colombia is based on Colombian Household Survey estimated by Cardenas and Montana (2020[35]); Kotera (2020[34]), "*How far will teleworking go?*"; Espinoza and Reznikova (2020[36]), "*Who can log in? The importance of skills for the feasibility of teleworking arrangements across OECD countries*".

Even before the outbreak of the pandemic, the Japanese Government had been promoting telework in order to create an environment that facilitates flexible work styles. For instance, in a 2017 Cabinet decision, the government undertook to triple the number of companies with teleworking practices by 2020 (compared to the number of firms of 2012). An ambitious government goal has been also set to double the number of employees benefitting from teleworking opportunities in 2022 compared with the fiscal year 2016 level (Cabinet Office, 2017[37]).

Efforts to promote flexible work practices were drastically hastened by the outbreak of the COVID-19 pandemic. In April 2020, the government encouraged companies to resort to telework in order to reduce attendance at office by at least 70%. In addition, in its "Emergency Economic Measures for New Coronavirus Infections" approved by the Cabinet in the same month, the government decided to expand support for the introduction of telework communication equipment in SMEs, as well as help the introduction of cybersecurity measures for SMEs. In particular, the Ministry of Health, Labour and Welfare (MHLW) implemented a subsidy scheme for SMEs covering 50% or up to JPY 1 million of the cost for purchasing ICT tools and operating a telework system. Use of the measure was substantial, with a total of more than 9 000 cases approved out of about 13 000 applications, and a total of JPY 3.52 billion has been paid as of October 2021 (averaging at JPY 380 000 per SME). The government also revised the "Guidelines for the Appropriate Introduction and Implementation of Teleworking Using Information and Communications Technology" on March 2021, in order to promote the successful implementation of teleworking systems and help employers and employees adjust to the new work styles of life during and after COVID-19.

In addition, the Ministry of Internal Affairs and Communications (MIC) expanded guidance on teleworking for managers. This programme was launched in 2016 to provide free advice on the introduction of teleworking practices by experts to companies and local government, and the experts have provided advice on ICT equipment for teleworking, information security, labour management, etc. In 2020, the number of consultants was increased from 21 to 109 in order to further promote the introduction of remote work practices during the COVID-19 crisis (Ministry of Internal Affairs and Communications, 2021[38]). Similarly, the Ministry of Economy, Trade and Industry (METI) launched the "SME Digitalization Support Team Project" – a programme providing SMEs with support for teleworking through advice on the use of digital tools by IT specialists.

Helped by the different policy measures taken by the Japanese Government during the COVID-19 crisis, the rate of teleworking in Japan jumped from 10% in December 2019 to 28% in May 2020 (Figure 2.10). By international comparison, Japan experienced the highest rise in teleworking practices in the OECD. However, Japan's teleworking rate was lower than that of Germany, Australia, France, and many other countries.

Figure 2.10. Japan's telework implementation surged in the wake of the pandemic

Increase in teleworking, during the COVID-19 pandemic compared to before

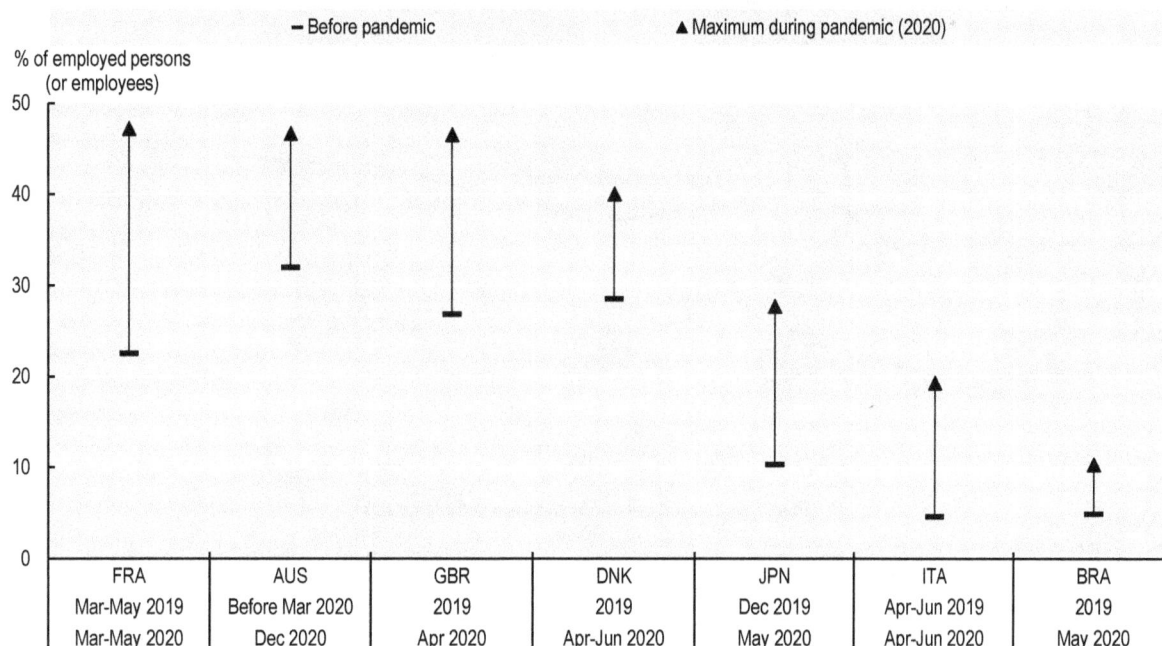

Note: AUS: share of employed persons working at home at least once in the last 4 weeks (self-reported). Before pandemic figure relates to "Before 1 March 2020", as reported in December 2020. Data relate to persons aged 18 years and over and come from the "Household impacts of COVID-19 survey". BRA: 2019 – percentage of (employed) people who usually worked from their homes. 2020 – percentage of (employed) people who worked from home in May 2020. It is important to mention that in the PNAD-COVID-19 questionnaire, the question that measures work at home explicitly asks about "teleworking" – whereas in the Continuous PNAD it is not. So, in part, the difference between the results can also be due to changes in the collection strategy. DNK: share of employed persons working at home at least once in the last 4 weeks (self-reported). Data relate to quarter 2 (March-June) and come from Labour Force Surveys. 2019 figure comes from the EU LFS dataset and relates to those teleworking "sometimes" or "usually". FRA: share of employed persons working at home in the period (self-reported). Data from INSEE enquêtes Emploi (employment surveys). GBR: share of employed persons "who did any working from home in the reference week". Estimated by the ONS using experimental Labour Market Survey datasets. ITA: share of employed persons working at home at least once in the last 4 weeks (self-reported). Data from the Labour Force Survey. JPN: Share of employed persons who answered "almost 100% teleworking", "mainly teleworking (more than 50%)", "mainly working at office (more than 50%) with occasional teleworking", or "basically working at office but teleworking irregularly" to the question regarding their working style using an ad-hoc "survey on changes in life consciousness and behaviour". Source: Criscuolo et al. (2021[39]), "The role of telework for productivity during and post-COVID-19: Results from an OECD survey among managers and workers", https://doi.org/10.1787/7fe47de2-en.

2.3.3. The COVID-19 pandemic widened the gap in telework implementation

While the implementation of teleworking expanded rapidly during the COVID-19 pandemic, significant disparities in telework practices have been observed among workers. For instance, Panel A of Figure 2.11 shows the percentage of workers who were teleworking at least partly at the time of the survey by region. While the gap between the telework implementation rate in Tokyo and in local rural areas was about 10 percentage points before the pandemic began, it expanded to about 30 percentage points during the crisis.

There are also large differences in telework implementation rates by firm size. As of 2019, the difference in implementation rates between large firms with more than 1 000 employees and small and medium-sized firms with less than 30 employees was 6 percentage points, but by 2021, the gap had widened to 26 percentage points (Panel B). This trend of increasing telework implementation rates with firm size is common in other OECD countries (Ker, Montagnier and Spiezia, 2021[40]). Finally, the gap between full-time workers and contract workers has also widened during the pandemic (Mugiyama, R and K. Komatsu, 2022[41]).

Figure 2.11. The implementation rate of teleworking has been increasing since COVID-19, but there is a large difference by region and firm size

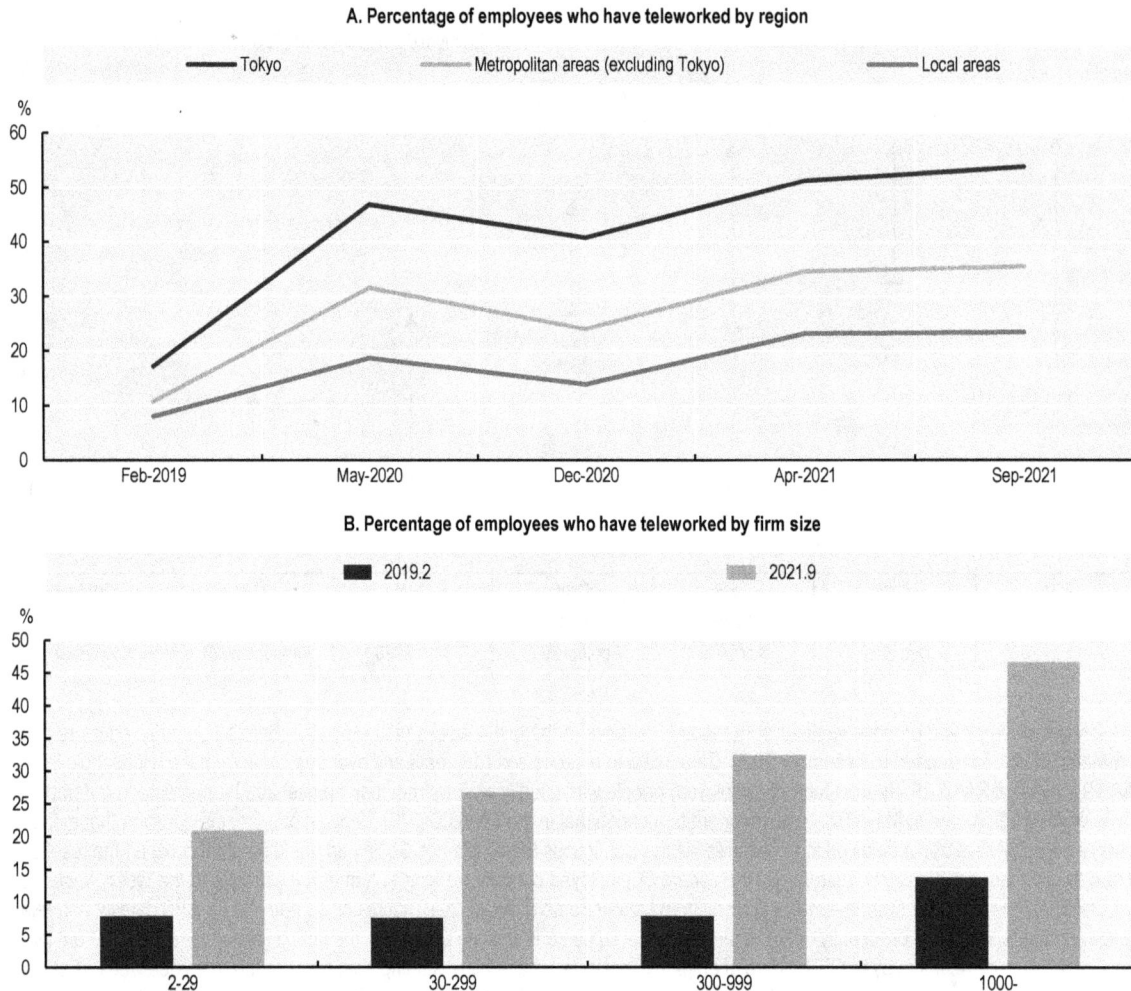

A. Percentage of employees who have teleworked by region

Tokyo — Metropolitan areas (excluding Tokyo) — Local areas

B. Percentage of employees who have teleworked by firm size

2019.2 — 2021.9

Note: Panel A. Metropolitan areas includes Saitama, Chiba, Kanagawa, Aichi, Gifu, Mie, Osaka, Kyoto, Hyogo, Shiga, Nara, and Wakayama Prefectures. Local areas are the 35 prefectures excluding Tokyo and Metropolitan areas.
Source: OECD calculation based on the Survey on Changes in Attitudes and Behaviours under the COVID-19 (Cabinet Office).

Not surprisingly, there are also large disparities by industry. Activities related to physical production or interactions, such as health care and social assistance, construction, transportation and warehousing, and accommodation and food services, have relatively low proportions of teleworkers across OECD countries, including France and the United States (Figure 2.12). In contrast, industries that are already highly digitised, such as information and communication services, professional and scientific services, and financial services, have very high teleworking rates, reaching well beyond 50%. While these trends are generally similar in Japan, one major difference is that the telework rate in the public sector is lower than in other countries, hence limiting the "lead by example" effect on private companies.

Figure 2.12. Differences in teleworking arise by industry

Teleworking peaks during the COVID-19 pandemic, by industry, 2020

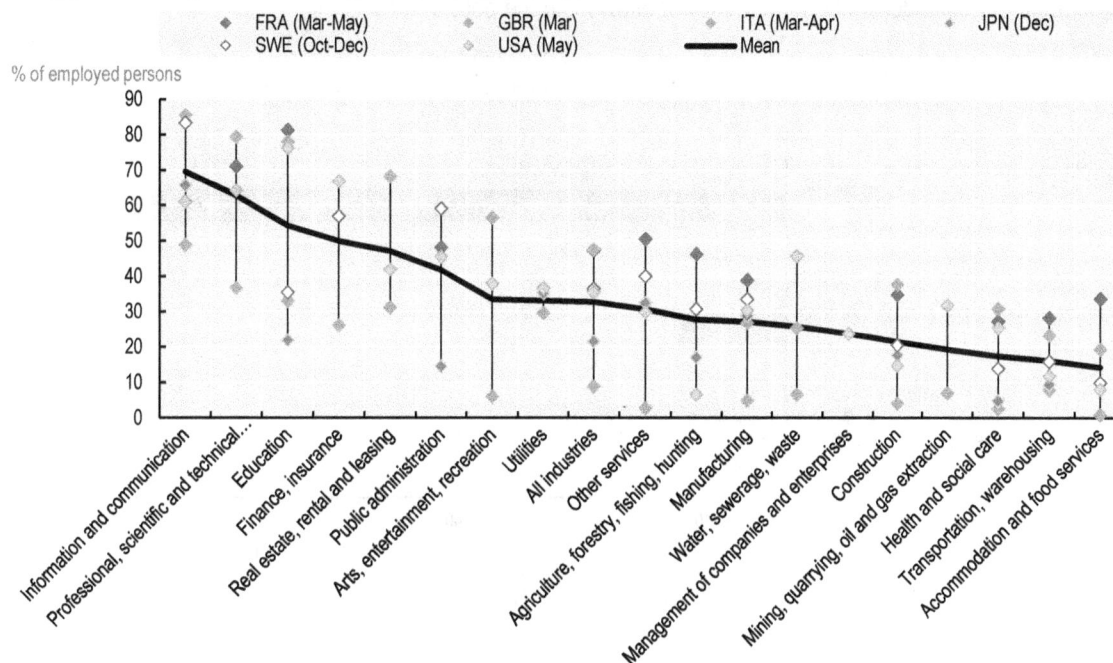

Note: The industry breakdown available varies and the alignment of industries across countries is approximate in some cases. Where some countries have more detail than others – for example, several countries separate retail trade and wholesale trade – the simple average is taken. FRA: share of employees teleworking or remote working in reporting week (firm-reported). GBR: share of employees working remotely instead of at their normal place of work in the last 2 weeks (firm-reported). ITA: share of employees remote or smart working in reporting period (firm-reported). JPN: data relate to "Telework" collected through an ad-hoc "survey on changes in life consciousness and behaviour". SWE: share of employed persons (aged 15-74) working at home at least once in the last 4 weeks (self-reported). USA: share of employed persons who teleworked or worked from home in the last 4 weeks because of the coronavirus pandemic (self-reported).
Source: Criscuolo et al. (2021[39]), "The role of telework for productivity during and post-COVID-19: Results from an OECD survey among managers and workers", https://doi.org/10.1787/7fe47de2-en.

The skills gap between different groups of workers, coupled with the fact that jobs requiring high skills already seem to be the most likely to have remote work practices, suggests that the prevalence of telework may exacerbate existing disparities in working conditions if not managed and mainstreamed properly. Indeed, a lack of targeted public policies ensuring the widespread application of flexible work arrangements (when possible) risks to further increase polarisation and inequality between older, higher-skilled workers with high incomes and typically employed by large firms, and younger workers with low incomes and low skills employed by small firms (Sostero, M. et al, 2020[42]).

There is also a large difference in perception of teleworking practices between those who have previously teleworked and those who have not. While 79% of the former are willing to telework at least one day per week after the COVID-19 pandemic, this percentage drops to 33% for those who have never teleworked before (Figure 2.13). Although it is possible that many of the non-teleworkers are mainly engaged in face-to-face work, and thus would have difficulty implementing telework, the results suggest that those who have implemented telework generally are positive about continuing to do so in the future.

Figure 2.13. The desired frequency of telework in the future varies greatly depending on whether or not there is teleworking experience

Percentage of respondents about frequency of telework in the post COVID-19

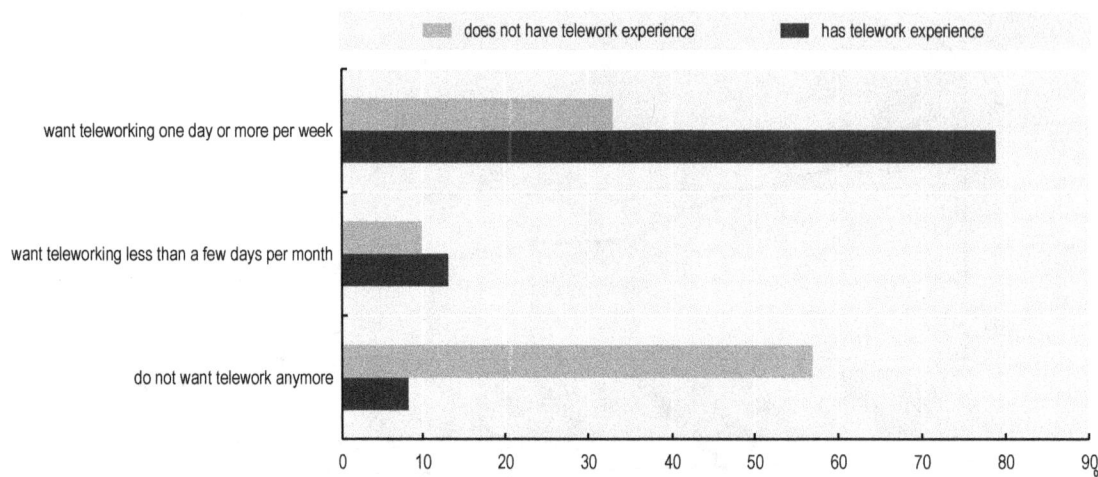

Source: Persol Research Institute, "Urgent survey on the impact of COVID-19 on telework".

2.3.4. Skill development and work styles need to be reviewed in order to maximise the potential of telework promotion implementation

Companies' practices such as corporate culture and evaluation methods also make a difference in the implementation rate of telework. A survey designed to examine working conditions before and after the declaration of a state of emergency shows that workplaces where people working overtime or working while on holiday are highly valued had significantly higher rates of in-presence work practices (Ishii, K. M. Nakayama and I. Yamamoto, 2021[43]). On the other hand, workplaces where the emphasis is on work performance and efficiency, or where there is a high degree of discretion such as "evaluations vary greatly according to performance" and "supervisors have a very flexible work style", have higher rates of teleworking. Encouraging the uptake of diverse working styles, while paying attention to limiting long working hours and improving work-life balance and health, would indirectly foster the diffusion of teleworking.

Looking at the relationship between skills and teleworking in the same survey, the higher the digital skills of employees, such as ability to work with spreadsheets and programming, the higher is the probability of teleworking. In addition, the higher the degree of adoption of new technology in the workplace, the more likely teleworking is to take root. This partly suggests that the degree of acceptance of new technology in the workplace and the improvement of IT skills of workers are important for the diffusion of telework. An international survey found that the perception that the quality of its ICT infrastructure hindered telework was most common in Japan among the OECD countries (Criscuolo et al., 2021[39]), though the results should be interpreted with some caution due to the small sample size. The government should develop policies to increase teleworking capacity and ICT skills of low-skilled workers and women in SMEs. Policies also need to support businesses and workers in accessing fast, reliable, and secure ICT infrastructure, with particular attention to SMEs and rural areas.

On the other hand, the introduction of teleworking may also require firms to implement company-wide systems and change business processes, rather than simply converting operations online. According to the survey on the teleworking population in 2021, although 80% of firms that have not introduced telework answered "there are no jobs suitable for telework", the other main reasons for not introducing teleworking included internal decision-making issues such as difficulties in progressing work (34%), corporate ICT issues such as cybersecurity risks (19%) digitalisation of documents (17%), difficulty of internal communication (10%) and the high cost involved (10%) (Ministry of Land, Infrastructure, Transport and Tourism, 2022[44]). It would be effective for the government not only to encourage firms in adopting digital tools such as teleconferencing systems and business chat tools, but also to accumulate and disseminate good examples on how to improve communication among employees.

The government should also play an important role in ensuring that the benefits of telework are not enjoyed only by highly skilled workers and companies with a high affinity for telework. As discussed above, skills upgrading and training on both hard and soft skills should be supported to increase the capacity of workers and managers. In addition, given that the implementation of teleworking also depends on the workers' degree of work discretion, it would be desirable for the government to provide support so that firms can smoothly review employees' work styles to increase their flexibility and focus on results and efficiency. Other countries are increasingly directing policy interventions toward networks rather than individual firms in order to improve workplace organisation. For instance, Finland, a pioneer in workplace innovation efforts, funded a learning network project to support joint learning forums consisting of researchers and businesses (OECD, 2020[45]). This initiative was based on the view that the most effective way of generating new innovative solutions for the working environment is a close co-operation and interaction between businesses, researchers, consultants, public authorities and social partners. A more recent programme, *Liideri* (Business, Productivity and Joy at Work Programme) focused in particular on developing management practices and forms of working that promote the active utilisation of the skills and competences of employees. A number of instruments are funded, including work organisation development projects, integrated R&D projects, funding for research, and widespread dissemination of the outcomes (OECD/ILO, 2017[46]).

Policy recommendations

Support employment retention

- Phase out special measures for employment adjustment subsidies gradually, taking into account the situation in the sectors affected by COVID-19, and shift the focus to policies to support labour mobility, such as upskilling and reskilling workers, and subsidising labour mobility from businesses that have downsized to growing industries.

- Improve the method of compiling data on employment adjustment subsidies by reviewing data collection forms in order to obtain more disaggregated data, such as data on the number of users of the subsidies, the characteristics of workers who received subsidies and the breakdown information by subsidy type.

- Assess the effectiveness of job retention schemes for protecting different types of workers from the risk of unemployment and for supporting longer-term career paths.

- Continue to promote the digitalisation of administrative services such as the online subsidy application system by spreading awareness about the tool and improving the digital infrastructure.

Support the digitalisation of career guidance services

- Promote career guidance services with more online opportunities for workers and support companies in introducing Self-Career Dock system through the Career Development Support Centre, which promotes and facilitates career guidance services.

- Provide basic digital skills programme for people who are less likely to receive online career guidance and teleworking, such as older age groups, non-regular workers and those living in rural areas so that career guidance and digitalisation of work practices are effective for all.

- Ensure that career guidance is not limited to online consultations, but also makes available a variety of digital tools, including emails and mobile messenger applications, in order to provide comprehensive support to those most removed from the labour market.

Fostering the adoption of teleworking practices

- Strengthen support for the introduction of teleworking particularly for small and medium-sized enterprises, where teleworking has not progressed, through public policies such as subsidies and consultation assistance.

- Support the expansion of more diverse work styles, such as regular employment with limited duties and regular employment with strong discretion in one's own work, which will facilitate the expansion of teleworking and workers' independent skills development.

- Collect and disseminate good practice examples about teleworking, including on how to improve communication among employees and how to ensure effective labour management, such as health management and working time management during teleworking.

- Improve work flexibility by further expanding the flextime system (flexible working arrangement) while paying attention to ensuring workers' health through setting work interval system and actively introduce ICT equipment in public sector workplaces to establish a system that enables those civil servants who wish to do so to telework.

References

Battiston, D., J. Blanes and T. Kirchmaier (2017), "Is Distance Dead? Face-to-Face Communication and Productivity in Teams", *CEPR Discussion Paper, No. 11924*, http://www.cepr.org. [28]

Beckmann, M., T. Cornelissen and M. Kräkel (2017), "Self-managed working time and employee effort: Theory and evidence", Vol. Vol. 133, https://doi.org/10.1016/j.jebo.2016.11.013. [21]

Beckmann, M. (2016), *Self-managed working time and firm performance: Microeconometric evidence", WWZ Working Paper, No. 2016/01, Center of Business and Economics, University of Basel.* [20]

Bloom, N. et al. (2015), "Does Working from Home Work? Evidence from a Chinese Experiment", *The Quarterly Journal of Economics*, Vol. Vol. 122/4, pp. pp. 1351-1408, https://doi.org/10.1093/qje/qju032. [23]

Bohns, V. (2017), "A Face-to-Face Request Is 34 Times More Successful Than an Email, Harvard Business Review", *Harvard Business Review*, https://hbr.org/2017/04/a-face-to-face-request-is-34-times-more-successful-than-an-email. [26]

Bonet, R. and F. Salvadora (2017), "When the boss is away: Manager-worker separation and worker performance in a multisite software maintenance organization", *Organization Science*, Vol. Vol. 28/2, pp. pp. 244-261, https://doi.org/10.1287/orsc.2016.1107. [29]

Cabinet Office (2022), "Japan Economy 2021-2022", https://www5.cao.go.jp/keizai3/2021/0207nk/pdf/n21_5.pdf. [1]

Cabinet Office (2021), "Japan Economy 2020-2021", https://www5.cao.go.jp/keizai3/2020/0331nk/keizai2020-2021pdf.html. [4]

Cabinet Office (2017), "the Basic Plan for the Creation of the World's Most Advanced IT Nation and the Promotion of Public-Private Data Utilization(世界最先端ＩＴ国家創造宣言・官民データ活用推進基本計画について)", https://www.kantei.go.jp/jp/singi/it2/kettei/pdf/20170530/siryou1.pdf. [37]

Cardenas, J. and J. Montana (2020), *Possible effects of Coronavirus in the Colombian labour market*, https://www.researchgate.net/profile/Jeisson-Cardenas/publication/341277637_Possible_effects_of_Coronavirus_in_the_Colombian_labour_market/links/5ec68724299bf1c09acff0bb/Possible-effects-of-Coronavirus-in-the-Colombian-labour-market.pdf. [35]

Cedefop (2020), *Inventory of lifelong guidance systems and practices - France*, https://www.cedefop.europa.eu/en/publications-and-resources/country-reports/inventory-lifelong-guidance-systems-and-practices-france#guidance-for-the-employed. [17]

Cedefop, European Commission, ETF, ILO, OECD, UNESCO (2021), *Investing in career guidance: Revised edition 2021*, https://www.etf.europa.eu/en/publications-and-resources/publications/investing-career-guidance. [16]

Clancy, M. (2020), "The Case for Remote Work", *Economics Working Papers, No. 20007, Iowa State University, Department of Economics*, https://dr.lib.iastate.edu/entities/publication/afaf9a36-d2e3-4c60-93b9-be40cdbd8993. [24]

Criscuolo, C. et al. (2021), "The role of telework for productivity during and post-COVID-19: Results from an OECD survey among managers and workers", *OECD Productivity Working Papers*, No. 31, OECD Publishing, Paris, https://doi.org/10.1787/7fe47de2-en. [39]

Department of Education and Skills (2020), "Continuity of Guidance Counselling: Guidelines for schools providing online support for students", https://www.ncge.ie/sites/default/files/schoolguideance/docs/continuity-of-guidancecounselling-. [18]

Dingel, J. and B. Neiman (2020), "How Many Jobs Can be Done at Home", *NBER Working Paper, No. 26948*, https://doi.org/10.3386/w26948. [33]

Espinoza, R. and L. Reznikova (2020), "Who can log in? The importance of skills for the feasibility of teleworking arrangements across OECD countries", *OECD Social, Employment and Migration Working Papers*, No. 242, OECD Publishing, Paris, https://doi.org/10.1787/3f115a10-en. [36]

Godart, O., H. Görg and A. Hanley (2017), *Trust-Based Work Time and Innovation: Evidence from Firm-Level Data", ILR Review, Vol. 70/4, pp. 894-918*, https://doi.org/10.1177/0019793916676259. [19]

Hovhannisyan, N. and W. Keller (2019), "International Business Travel and Technology Sourcing", *NBER Working Paper*, Vol. No. 25862, https://doi.org/10.3386/w25862. [30]

Ishii, K. M. Nakayama and I. Yamamoto (2021), "Potential benefits and retention potential of teleworking at Corona Disaster: . Verification using panel data(コロナ禍での在宅勤務の潜在的メリットと定着可能性：パネルデータを用いた検証)", *Panel Data Research Center, Keio University PDRC Discussion Paper Series*, https://www.pdrc.keio.ac.jp/uploads/DP2021-007_jp.pdf. [43]

Japan Manpower (2021), "Survey Results of Qualified National Career Consultants (Year 2) (国家資格キャリアコンサルタント有資格者調査結果（2年目）)", https://www.nipponmanpower.co.jp/cc/tps_details/LDWIKE4R/. [14]

Ker, D., P. Montagnier and V. Spiezia (2021), "Measuring telework in the COVID-19 pandemic", *OECD Digital Economy Papers*, No. 314, OECD Publishing, Paris, https://doi.org/10.1787/0a76109f-en. [40]

Kotera, S. (2020), "How far will teleworking go? (在宅勤務はどこまで進むか)", https://www.mizuho-ir.co.jp/publication/mhri/research/pdf/insight/jp200522.pdf. [34]

Ministry of Health, Labour and Welfare (2022), *雇用調整助成金（新型コロナウイルス感染症の影響に伴う特例）(Subsidy for employment adjustment (Special exception due to the impact of new coronavirus infection).* [7]

Ministry of Health, Labour and Welfare (2021), *2021 Labour Economics Analysis*, https://www.mhlw.go.jp/wp/hakusyo/roudou/20/dl/20-2.pdf. [2]

Ministry of Internal Affairs and Communications (2021), "Task Force to Study the State of Teleworking in the 'Post-COVID-19' Era, Secretariat document", https://www.soumu.go.jp/main_content/000748246.pdf. [38]

Ministry of Land, Infrastructure, Transport and Tourism (2022), *Results of the survey on the teleworking population in FY2021*. [44]

Monteiro, N. (2019), "Does remote work improve or impair firm labour productivity? Longitudinal evidence from Portugal", *NIPE Working Paper*. [22]

Morikawa, M. (2021), "Productivity of Working from Home during the COVID-19 Pandemic: Evidence from a Firm Survey", *Discussion papers 21002, Research Institute of Economy, Trade and Industry (RIETI)*. [25]

Mugiyama, R and K. Komatsu (2022), "Disparities in Telework Enability: The Time-series comparison before and after a new coronavirus outbreak(テレワーク実施可能性における格差：新型コロナウイルス感染症流行前後の時系列比較)", https://www.jil.go.jp/tokusyu/covid-19/dp/202203/docs/DP3.pdf. [41]

OECD (2022), "Leveraging career guidance for adults to build back better", *OECD Policy Responses to Coronavirus (COVID-19)*, OECD Publishing, Paris, https://doi.org/10.1787/ab7e7894-en. [15]

OECD (2022), *OECD Employment Outlook 2022: Building Back More Inclusive Labour Markets*, OECD Publishing, Paris, https://doi.org/10.1787/1bb305a6-en. [5]

OECD (2022), "Riding the waves: Adjusting job retention schemes through the COVID-19 crisis", *OECD Policy Responses to Coronavirus (COVID-19)*, OECD Publishing, Paris, https://doi.org/10.1787/ae8f892f-en. [6]

OECD (2021), *Career Guidance for Adults in a Changing World of Work*, Getting Skills Right, OECD Publishing, Paris, https://doi.org/10.1787/9a94bfad-en. [11]

OECD (2021), *Creating Responsive Adult Learning Opportunities in Japan*, Getting Skills Right, OECD Publishing, Paris, https://doi.org/10.1787/cfe1ccd2-en. [12]

OECD (2021), *OECD Economic Surveys: Japan 2021*, OECD Publishing, Paris, https://doi.org/10.1787/6b749602-en. [9]

OECD (2021), *OECD Employment Outlook 2021: Navigating the COVID-19 Crisis and Recovery*, OECD Publishing, Paris, https://doi.org/10.1787/5a700c4b-en. [3]

OECD (2020), "Job retention schemes during the COVID-19 lockdown and beyond", *OECD Policy Responses to Coronavirus (COVID-19)*, OECD Publishing, Paris, https://doi.org/10.1787/0853ba1d-en. [10]

OECD (2020), "Productivity gains from teleworking in the post COVID-19 era: How can public policies make it happen?", *OECD Policy Responses to Coronavirus (COVID-19)*, OECD Publishing, Paris, https://doi.org/10.1787/a5d52e99-en. [31]

OECD (2020), *Workforce Innovation to Foster Positive Learning Environments in Canada*, Getting Skills Right, OECD Publishing, Paris, https://doi.org/10.1787/a92cf94d-en. [45]

OECD/ILO (2017), *Better Use of Skills in the Workplace: Why It Matters for Productivity and Local Jobs*, Local Economic and Employment Development (LEED), OECD Publishing, Paris, https://doi.org/10.1787/9789264281394-en. [46]

Ohta, S., Y. Genda and A. Kondo (2008), "The Endless Ice Age: A Review of the Cohort Effect in Japan", *Japanese Economy, Vol. 35/3*, pp. pp. 55-86, https://doi.org/10.2753/jes1097-203x350303.　[8]

Ozimek, A. (2020), "The Future of Remote Work", https://www.upwork.com/press/releases/the-future-of-remote-work.　[32]

Roghanizad, M. and V. Bohns (2017), "Ask in person: You're less persuasive than you think over email", *Journal of Experimental Social Psychology*, Vol. Vol. 69, pp. pp. 223-226, https://doi.org/10.1016/j.jesp.2016.10.002.　[27]

Sostero, M. et al (2020), "Teleworkability and the COVID-19 Crisis: a New Digital Divide?", *JRC Working Paper Series on Labour, Education and Technology, No. 2020/05*, https://ec.europa.eu/jrc/sites/default/files/jrc121193.pdf.　[42]

The Japan Institute for Labor Policy Training (2022), "先進各国のキャリア関連資格及びキャリア支援のオンライン化に関する研究(Research on career-related qualifications and online career support in developed countries)", https://www.jil.go.jp/institute/siryo/2022/250.html.　[13]

Notes

[1] Based on information as of December 2021 except for Japan.

[2] The Career Development Support centres provide career consulting services to workers, support the introduction of the Self-Career Dock system, and provide assistance to companies that utilise the job card system (a form of CV that summarises a person's professional experience, qualifications and certificates, as well as training and learning records and work performance evaluations). Through these efforts, their mission is to support the autonomous career development of workers and improve companies' productivity. The centres were established in April 2020, reorganising and integrating the previously existing Job Card centres.

3 Looking ahead: Innovative skills policies for a strong recovery

Japan needs to ensure that upskilling and reskilling policies are targeted, inclusive, and based on a more systematic analysis of labour market developments. This chapter reviews how Japan has adapted its adult learning policies after the outbreak of the COVID-19 pandemic, and explores the need for digital, modular, and flexible training opportunities. Furthermore, the chapter emphasises the need of better leveraging existing data to create analytical tools to assess and anticipate skills needs to enable decision makers to quickly adapt training offers and career guidance services to the evolving world of work.

In Brief

Japan needs to ensure that upskilling and reskilling policies are targeted, inclusive, and based on more systematic analysis of labour market developments

Japan was quick to react to the pandemic, and many training courses were adjusted to face the new realities of social distancing and teleworking. Though training programmes for both employed and unemployed adults have increased in number and become easier to access, large gaps in skills use and training persist. In Japan, women are employed in occupations that involve limited leadership skills such as co-ordination, problem solving and high-level decision making, and they participate less in job-related training compared to men. Non-regular workers are working in occupations with lower skill demands and display a large gap in training participation compared to regular workers. Recent adult learning reforms have not fully addressed these gaps.

To move the needle on adult learning in Japan, digital, modular and flexible training opportunities that address the gaps in participation are needed. Digitalisation and online provision can increase the availability of training and circumvent many of the time constraints that adults in Japan face. Modularisation, micro-credentials and tailored training programmes can increase participation by offering shorter courses that can be stacked together over time to achieve a recognised qualification, and are better aligned with local labour market needs and the skills and experience of the adult learner.

Employment outcomes of participants in Japan's public training programmes is relatively high. However, there is room to improve public vocational training and align better to changing skill needs. Building better labour market information systems will help identify changes in the labour market and skill needs in real time, allowing policy makers to quickly adapt training offerings and career guidance services. The adult learning market in Japan can be further expanded by creating a virtuous circle of adults' participation in training by linking a good labour market information system with the provision of appropriate training and career guidance.

3.1. Differences in skill level and training participation between socio-demographic groups in Japan ·

As discussed in previous chapters, not only did the COVID-19 pandemic change the composition of skills in the Japanese labour market, but it also triggered a range of policy responses from the government intended to increase labour market flexibility and withstand shocks. These initiatives were introduced to respond to a sudden and immediate crisis and they contributed to the longer-term trends towards digitalisation and teleworking experienced across OECD countries. However, more efforts to ensure a strong and sustainable recovery are needed, with more attention devoted to specific segments of the population.

3.1.1. There are large differences in skill level between demographic groups in Japan

The analysis of the skill composition in Japan presented in Chapter 1 suggested that the Japanese economy requires high levels of foundation and social skills – indicators of a knowledge-based economy. When the same analysis is carried out for different demographic groups, it becomes evident that there are important differences in skill requirements faced by socio-demographic groups in the Japanese population. Figure 3.1 shows that men and women in the workforce hold jobs with approximately the same level of high-frequency skills (such as foundational skills) and low-frequency skills (such as knowledge of foreign skills). However, women in the workforce are also more likely than men to be employed in occupations with lower levels of most social skills, as well as lower levels of advance cognitive skills (i.e. time management and complex problem solving skills).

On average, relative to men, women are employed in jobs that involve less leadership, less responsibility, where they do not carry out tasks that require high levels of co-ordination, problem solving and high-level decision making. The higher level of understanding of other people's reactions and interpersonal support services could be a reflection of women traditionally dominating in customer-facing occupations such as hospitality. Women are also employed in occupations with lower levels of technical skills than men. This is likely caused by gender stereotyping in service-related occupations and provides a policy opportunity for the government. Information campaigns, career guidance and female role-models in education could help boost female employment in male-dominated professions.

Figure 3.1. Women hold jobs with lower requirements in social, technical and high-level decision making skills

Skills composition indicator (scale 1-7)

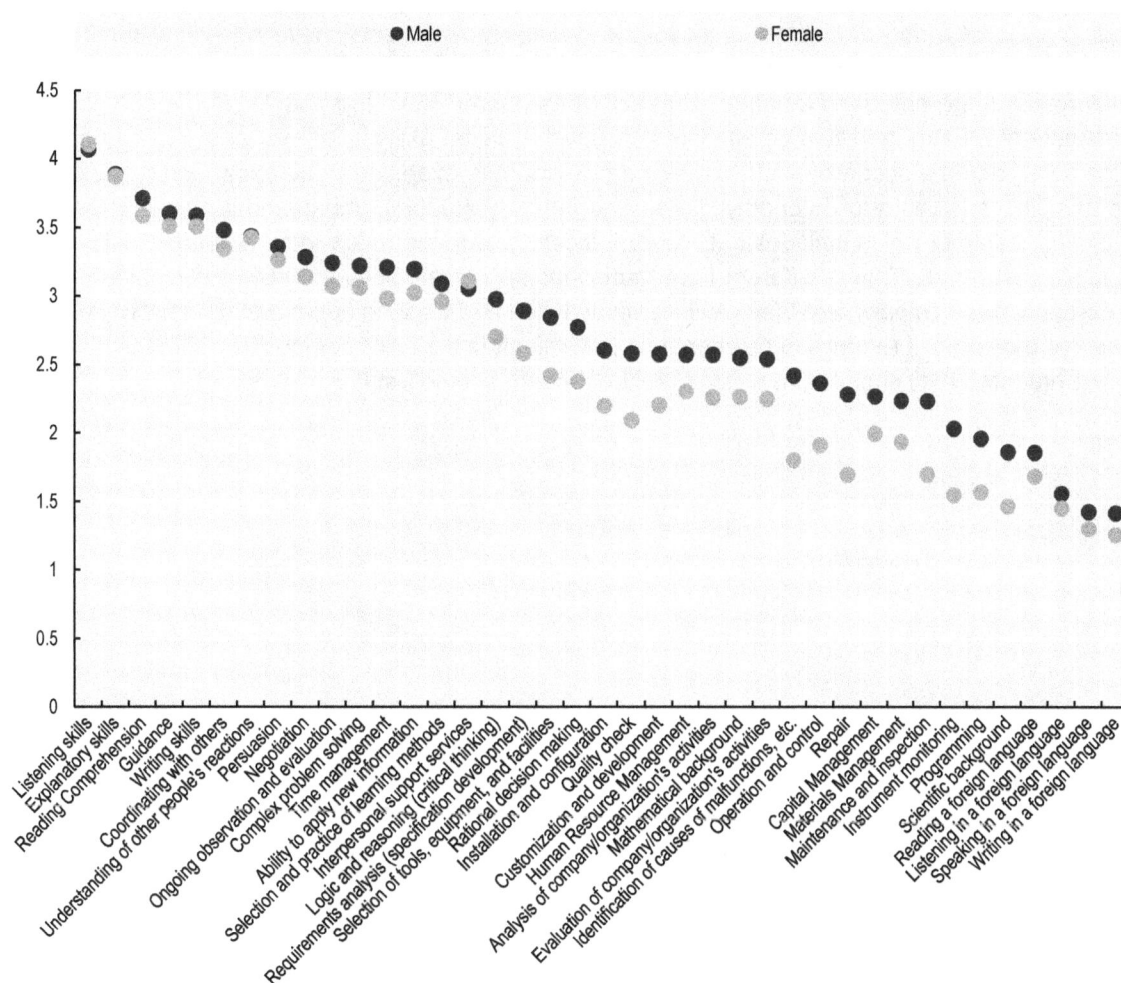

Note: The Skills Composition Indicator is calculated using a weighted average, taking into account both skill level of occupation and number of people working in that occupation, and it is calculated by multiplying each skill level for a given occupation with the number of workers in that occupation, and then dividing by the total number of workers in the data set. The sample includes employees between 20 and 65 years old. The full scale for skill level ranges from 0 to 7, but has been shortened to 0-5 to better present the data.
Source: Japanese Panel Study of Employment Dynamics and Japanese O*NET survey.

Unlike women who are less likely to work in leadership positions requiring high social and advance cognitive skills but are as present as men in occupations using high levels of foundation skills, non-regular workers generally hold lower-skilled occupations. Indeed, non-regular workers (temporary contract) are employed in occupations with lower skill levels for all skills when compared to regular workers (permanent contract) (Figure 3.2). Among non-regular workers, those with part-time contracts are in occupations using skills at lower levels than those in non-regular full-time contracts. This is a reflection of two aspects of the Japanese labour market: i) there is a higher instance of non-regular workers in low-skilled occupations; and ii) there is little investment in training and development for non-regular workers meaning there is little innovation and skill increase in positions filled by non-regular workers.

Recently, the Japanese Government passed legislation intending to address some of the gaps between regular and non-regular workers, and full-time and part-time workers. For instance, the Act on Improvement of Personnel Management and Conversion of Employment Status for Part-Time Workers and Fixed-Term Workers came into effect in April 2020 for companies with over 300 employees, and April 2021 for companies with over 100 employees, and prohibits unreasonable disparities between the treatment of regular employees and part-time/non-regular workers (Ministry of Health, Labour and Welfare, 2018[1]). Placing the responsibility of fair treatments of non-regular workers on employers, the law seeks to increase job security and rights of these workers, including training rights.

Though traditional forms of lifetime employment (permanent contracts) have been the dominant work contract in Japan, especially for men (OECD, 2021[2]), Following the pandemic-induced digital transformation there has been a shift in contract types offered to young people. Some companies now require new graduates and mid-career hires to have a digital skillset for key positions via "job-based employment", and the scope of such forms of employment is expected to be expanded to include other types of skillsets (Ministry of Economy, Trade and Industry, 2020[3]). Job-based employment entails an employment contract which includes duties, work location, working hours, etc., and the employees work only within that range. This is different from traditional lifetime employment in which employees devote their career to one company and their work location, duties and working hours are not narrowly prescribed and evolve over time. It remains to be seen how this will affect the skills composition of the labour market, as hiring practices may change towards more independent and self-sufficient workers.

Figure 3.2. Non-regular (temporary) workers are employed in generally lower-skilled jobs

Skills composition indicator (scale 1-7)

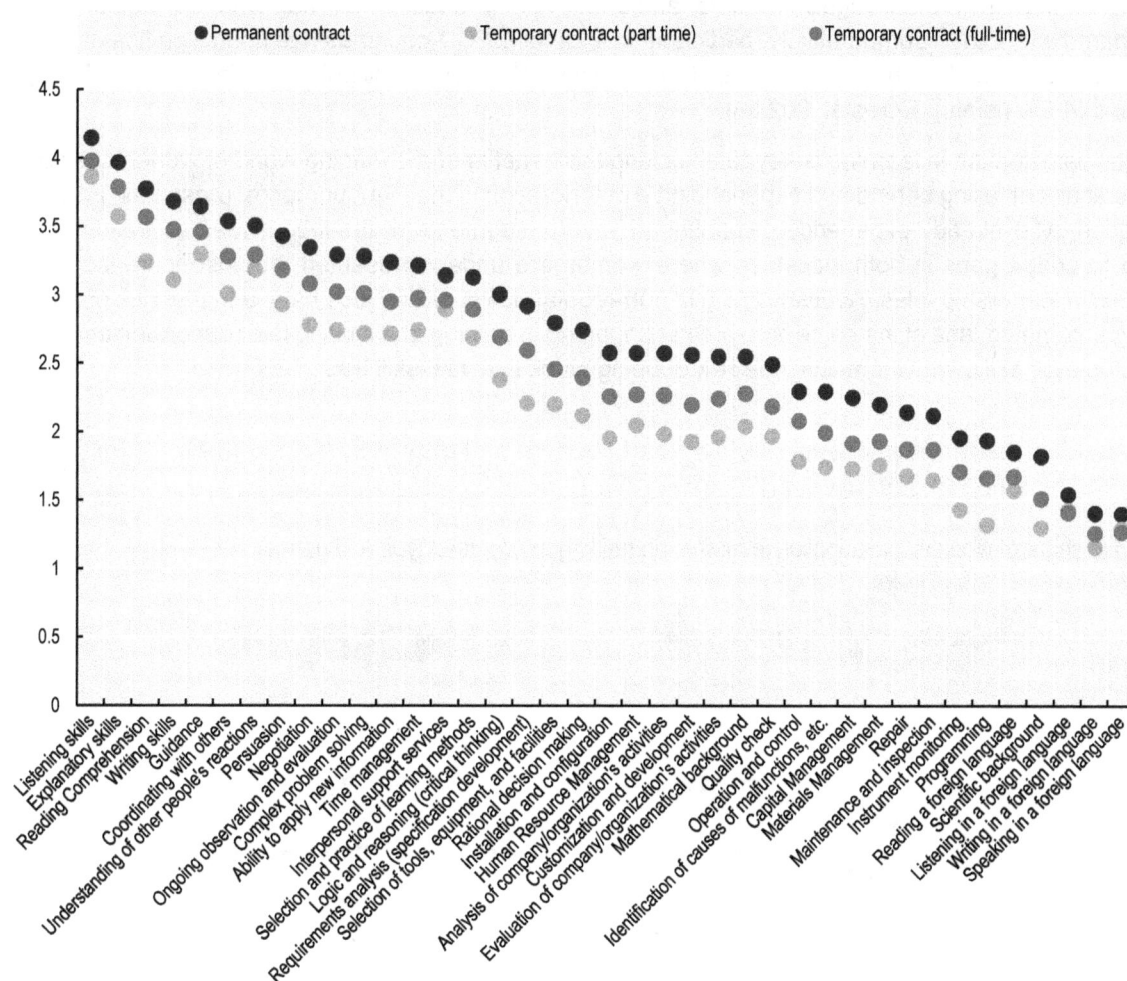

Note: The Skills Composition Indicator is calculated using a weighted average, taking into account both skill level of occupation and number of people working in that occupation, and it is calculated by multiplying each skill level for a given occupation with the number of workers in that occupation, and then dividing by the total number of workers in the data set. The sample includes employees between 20 and 65 years old. The full scale for skill level ranges from 0 to 7, but has been shortened to 0-5 to better present the data.
Source: Japanese Panel Study of Employment Dynamics and Japanese O*NET survey.

3.1.2. Changes in training policies are not been adequately addressing skills gaps

Job-related training is a policy tool that can be used to address and minimise skills gaps in the labour market. A well-designed training system takes into account changes in the demand for skills, availability of skills in the labour market, inequalities and barriers, as well as strategic planning for economic growth and labour market developments. Though many adults could benefit from upskilling and reskilling through training, there are large gaps in participation between both women and men, and regular and non-regular workers in Japan (Figure 3.3). Men in regular contracts train more than all other demographic groups, with a 40% participation rate in 2020. The group that follows in terms of the training participation rate is women in regular contracts (32%), men in non-regular contracts (20%), and the group with the lowest participation rate is women in non-regular contracts (15%). Both men (regular workers and non-regular workers) and women non-regular workers exhibited to a large extent the same trends in participation in training, namely a very slight increase in participation between 2010 and 2019 ranging from between 1.1 to 2% points. The training participation of women regular workers increased by over 5% points in the same period. However, participation dropped for all groups during the first year of the pandemic, ranging from a reduction of 5.5% points for women who are regular workers, and a 6.7% point reduction for men who are regular workers, compared with 2019. Comparatively, participation in other OECD countries has risen significantly more in the last decade (2012-19), e.g. in France (13.8% points), Sweden (7.3% points), Ireland (5.1% points) and Finland (4.5% points) (Eurostat, 2021[4]).

Adults' participation in learning is key to unlocking the benefits of a changing world of work, especially for those at risk of falling behind and experiencing a deterioration in their labour market prospects. For women in Japan, who already experience disparities in several segments of the labour market, training can be used to bridge gaps in both industries where women are underrepresented, but also increase hiring of women in leadership roles. Adults working in non-regular, lower skilled jobs have a higher risk of their jobs being automated, and at the same time are not engaging in training and limiting their opportunities to further develop their skills, and increasing the risk of being stuck in a 'low-skill trap'.

Figure 3.3. Prior to the pandemic, training participation had only increased moderately for men and non-regular workers, but has decreased for all groups since the pandemic

Trend in share of workers' participation in off-the-job training, by contract type and gender

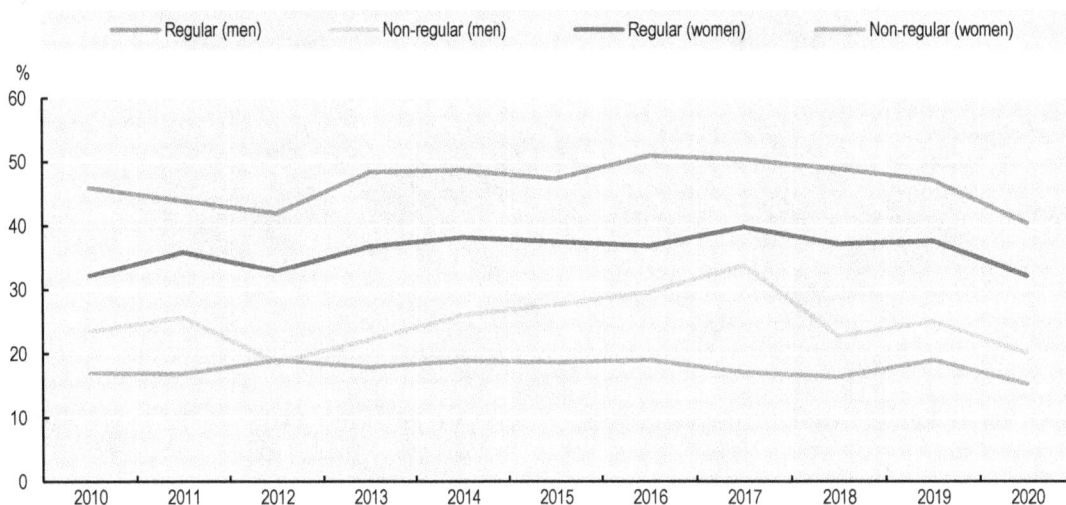

Note: The questionnaire question asks "What kind of OFF-JT training did you participate in?" (Multiple choice). Rate of participation is calculated by subtracting the option "I did not participate in OFF-JT" from the total.
Source: Basic Survey of Human Resources.

Since the outbreak of the pandemic, it has become even more apparent that adult learning is an important policy lever to adjust to changing work modes and styles. Throughout the pandemic, the increase in the number of infections and the measures to contain the spread of the virus, including stay-at-home requirements, also affected vocational training provision and participation. During the first wave of the outbreak, the government forced the public vocational training operators to close facilities where coronavirus infections among training participants took place, and to consider preventive closure even in the absence of infections.

Shortly after the first cases of the virus in Japan, the negative impacts on training became visible. Compared to 2019, vocational training for the unemployed remained largely unchanged, but for the employed, the number of people that undertook training in 2020 was 40% lower than in 2019 (Figure 3.4).

In Japan, public vocational training for both job seekers and employed workers is conducted at public training facilities administered by the national and prefectural governments. As discussed in detail in Section 3.3.1, the number of people eligible for training (for unemployed adults and workers) is determined according to the size of the budget after discussions at a council of interested parties each year, and detailed in a "National Vocational Training Implementation Plan". Following this, each prefecture draws up a plan for its own prefecture to be consistent with those figures (Ministry of Internal Affairs and Communications, 2016[5]). There is an established system whereby if there is an urgent need to increase training for job seekers, it is possible to reduce the scale of training offered to employed workers. During the pandemic, the number of working participants dropped due to containment measures (before courses pivoted to online delivery), while participation for job seekers remained the same, as the training providers prioritised this group.

Figure 3.4. Reduced training opportunities due to COVID-19 affected mostly employees

Changes in public vocational training enrolment

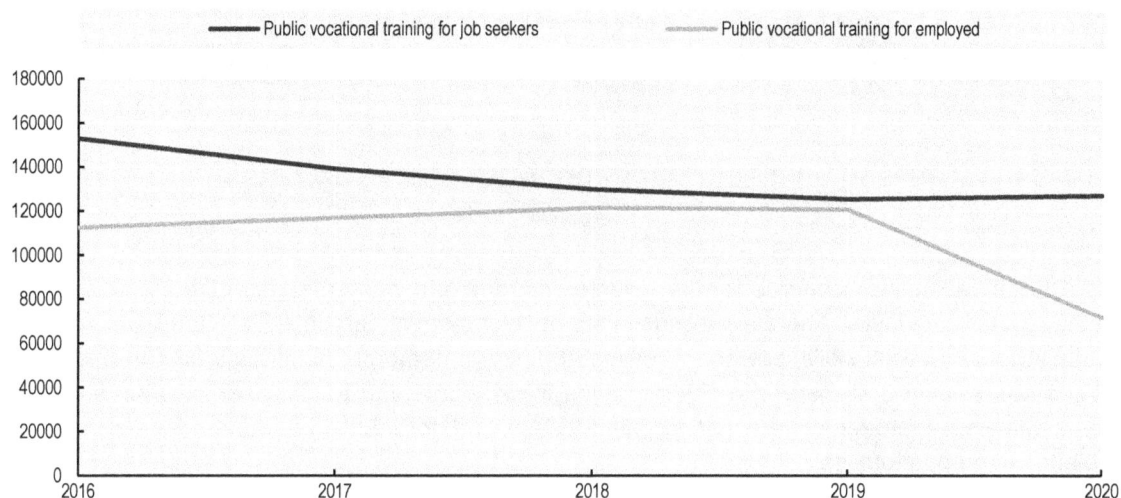

Note: Training for job seekers includes public job training and job seeker support training (mainly short-term training for those who cannot receive employment insurance).
Source: OECD Questionnaire on Policy Responses to the COVID-19 crisis.

Among jobseekers who attended public vocational training, participants in the clerical field account for about 30% of the total, making it the field with the largest number of participants in public vocational training. The next largest share of training is in IT and other information-related fields, at about 23% (Panel A of Figure 3.5). Looking at the number of trainees by age group, trainees are clustered in the 25-54 age group, with the 25-34 age group having the largest number of trainees. The number of participants in public vocational training declines sharply after the age of 55 (Panel B of Figure 3.5). There has been very little change in the composition of publicly provided vocational training, by field or by age of participants over the past five years.

Figure 3.5. The share of participants in public vocational training by field remains stable

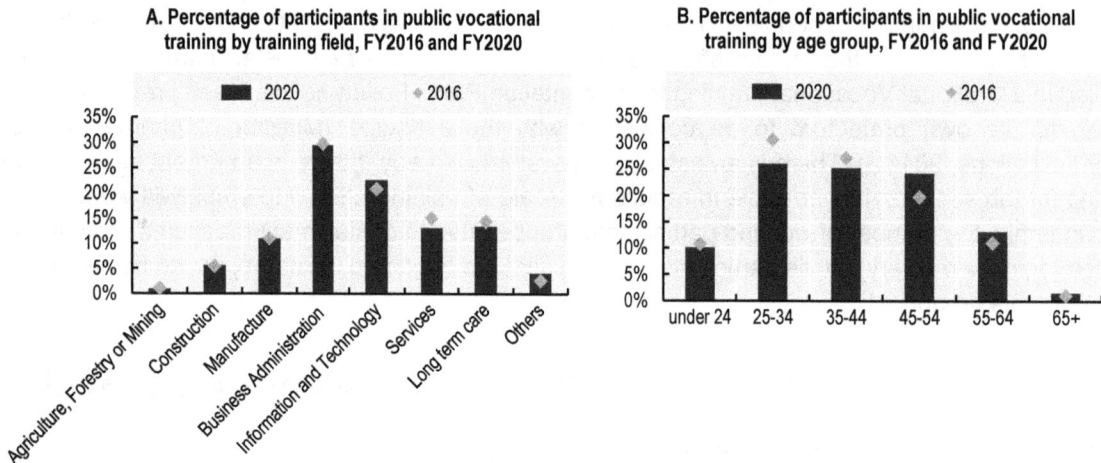

A. Percentage of participants in public vocational training by training field, FY2016 and FY2020

B. Percentage of participants in public vocational training by age group, FY2016 and FY2020

Note: Number of participants is the sum of those continuing from the previous year and those who entered the public vocational training. For Panel B, the number is the sum of public vocational training and the Support System for Job Seekers.
Source: OECD Questionnaire on Policy Responses to the COVID-19 crisis.

3.2. Digital, modular and flexible training opportunities to increase participation in adult learning

As illustrated, the Japanese workforce is very diverse with different workers using different skill sets to carry out their job-related tasks. There are trends in the development of certain skills in the labour market, such as analytical and social skills, but when looking at different demographic groups and work contract types it becomes evident that there is a diversification in skills use and training participation in Japan. Therefore, a universal approach of "one size fits all" does not work for adults. Learners need personalised and flexible training opportunities.

Online distance learning has the potential to address many of the barriers to adult learning. It allows learners to choose a time, pace and place that is compatible with their professional and personal responsibilities, and is often cheaper than equivalent face-to-face training. As shown in the context of the current COVID-19 crisis, online learning also has the potential to provide continuity when face-to-face training is not available. However, inclusiveness is a major concern when addressing online learning, as on one hand, online courses could facilitate access to training for adults with disabilities or those living in rural communities, but on the other hand, it requires basic digital skills and devices, as well as reliable internet infrastructure (OECD, 2020[6]). Investing in digital skills learning and infrastructure is crucial to the digitalisation of training. Therefore, in order for online training to be successful, broader training policy changes will need to accompany the digitalisation of learning.

As found by OECD (2021[2]), lack of time and scheduling constraints play a large role in Japan. The main reasons for not participating are a lack of time due to work responsibilities (29%), a lack of time due to child care or family responsibilities (27%), and the training taking place at an inconvenient time or place (19%). Despite its potential, data at the onset of the pandemic suggests that few adults took advantage of online learning as a means of training. Government data show that only around 4 700 job seekers were enrolled in government-funded online public vocational training in FY 2020. The low uptake of online learning is also due to low provision of online learning courses. For public vocational training, real-time interactive online training courses were introduced in May 2020. For the *Support System for Job Seekers*, real-time online interactive training courses have been available since February 2021, and on-demand (recorded) training courses have been available since October 2021. In part due to these changes and the better accessibility of online training opportunities, the number of participants in online public job training exceeded 10 000 in 2021, less than 1% of the total labour force. For the *Support System for Job Seekers,* only 1 000 people participated in online courses in 2021 (Figure 3.6).

Figure 3.6. Online course training enrolment is growing but remains low

Number of job seekers who participated in online public vocational training

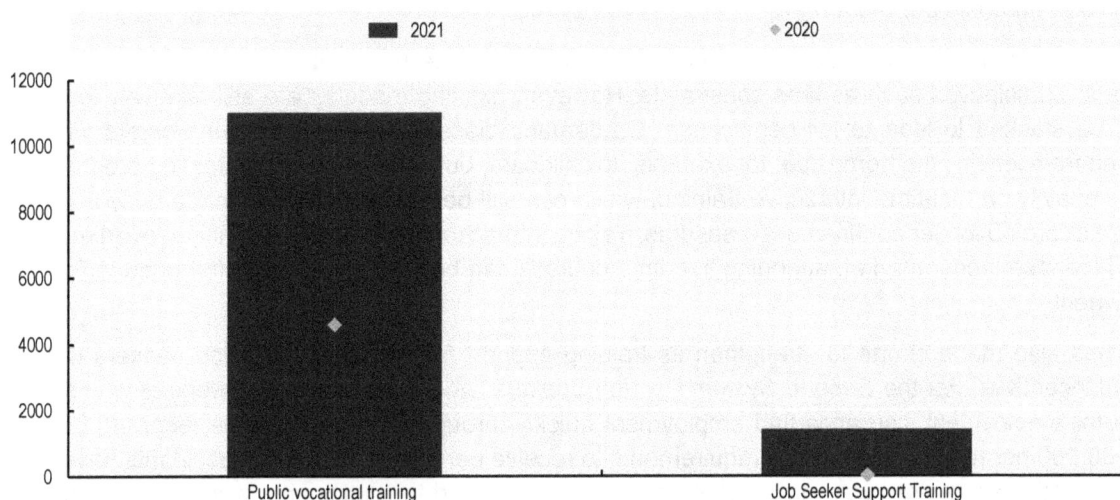

Note: The Number is the sum of on-demand and simultaneous interactive online training.
Source: OECD Questionnaire on Policy Responses to the COVID-19 crisis.

Online distance learning is just one piece of the puzzle when it comes to flexible learning. Low-skilled adults are less willing to participate in time-intensive training compared to high-skilled adults, not least due to the different preferences and personality traits of the two groups and the fact that low-skilled adults are likely to have lower digital skills (Fouarge, Schils and de Grip, 2012[7]). In this context, modular learning, whether online or in person, is the key in increasing training participation, as it allows adults to learn at their own pace. In contrast to traditional learning programmes, which must be completed in full to obtain a qualification, modular learning breaks up courses into self-contained modules. In the best-practice systems, each module has its own distinct learning outcomes, which are certified as partial credits or qualifications once completed. Students can study to get a full qualification over time, by adding more modules to their learning portfolio. In Flanders (Belgium), formal adult education is provided by the Centres for Adult Education (*Centra voor Volwassenonderwijs, CAE*), where all courses are modular and flexible (e.g. evening courses) (European Commission/EACEA/Eurydice, 2021[8]). After completing a module, the student receives a partial certification, and after completing a programme (composed of several modules) the student receives a formal certification recognised by the government. Graduates also receive a tuition reimbursement upon graduation. Further, the Flemish Government incentivises the Centres for Adult Education to provide distance learning by offering systematic direct financial support for training providers with programmes where at least 50% or the content is provided through distance learning.

Some improvements were made in Japan by shortening the length of training courses during the pandemic. For public vocational training, the standard training period used to be minimum three months, but during the pandemic, courses that last one or two months were established and the minimum training hours to qualify for financial support were reduced from 100 hours to 60 hours. This made the course more accessible to employed people, who often face time constraints in participating in training. Courses with reduced durations were established in a wide range of fields, such as training and exercises for the care and welfare industry (66-hour course), training on security engineer training and information system operation and maintenance for the IT industry (60-hour course), training for salespersons who are authorised to sell pharmaceutical products (60-hour course), and training to learn and practice how to operate machines for the construction industry (60-hour course).

For the *Training in support of Job Seekers,* the minimum length of training programmes was reduced from two months to two weeks, thereby enabling people to participate in different types of training over a shorter period of time. In addition, the minimum training hours to qualify for financial support were lowered from 100 hours to 60 hours per month.

Reducing the length and intensity of training courses can increase their uptake, as it tackles important barriers to participation such as time constraints. However, existing modules are still relatively long and cannot be stacked to lead to full certification. On-demand classes are available for workers who are restricted from leaving the home due, for example, to childcare, but most of the other training programmes still rely heavily on real-time interactive training, which can still be a challenge to fit into a busy schedule when there are no longer confinement measures. Taking into account the heavy reliance of overtime work in the Japanese labour market, attending live-time courses can be very challenging for those in full-time employment.

Japan has also made efforts to strengthen its training support for employers and job seekers through financial incentives. For the *Support System For Job Seekers,* where job seekers or workers who are not eligible for employment insurance find employment quickly through job training while receiving benefits (JPY 100 000 per month), the income requirements to receive benefits for training participants have been relaxed. Before the system was revised, job training benefits paid to participants were only available to those whose monthly income was JPY 80 000 or less (if they were employed at the time of training), but as a special temporary measure for those who work in shifts or have a second or dual job, the upper wage ceiling has been increased to JPY 120 000 per month. In addition, the attendance requirement for receiving benefits was relaxed (from 100% attendance except in unavoidable reasons such as sickness to 80% or more attendance) to make it easier for those working during training to receive benefits. Table 3.1 summarises the main programme reforms that have taken place during the pandemic.

Table 3.1. Training policy review focused on improving access to training

Training policies revision in response to COVID-19

	The Support System for Job Seekers	Public Vocational Training
Training Period	Relaxed from 2 months to 6 months to 2 weeks to 6 months	New courses of 1 to 2 months were established instead of 3 months.
Training Hours	Course length shortened from 100 hours or more to 60 hours or more per month.	Course length shortened from 100 hours per month to 60 hours or more per month
Relaxed income and attendance requirements for benefits	Relaxed income and attendance requirements for benefits	–
Online training	Facilitate setting up online training	Facilitate setting up online training

Source: Based on the "New Employment and Training Package" by the Ministry of Health, Labour and Welfare (2021).

While there has been progress on the fronts outlined above, little changes were made to target groups, delivery models or channels, and support for sectoral and occupational reallocation. In the 30 OECD countries for which information is available, about 30% changed the target groups of the training programmes, about 70% changed their delivery models or channels, and about 40% made to support sectoral and occupational reallocation – see Chapter 2 of OECD (2022[9]). Though several actions have been taken to improve labour market conditions for vulnerable groups with poorer labour market performance, such as requiring equal treatment of regular and non-regular workers and companies' reporting on gender equality plans, there have been no targeted measures for these groups with respects to training. As the Japanese labour market is being shaped by global megatrends and the pandemic, underserving those who are already falling behind risks increasing the gap further, making later intervention more costly. Utilising the momentum that has built during the pandemic, where stakeholders have a higher need and willingness to reform, is crucial to ensure that the Japanese labour force has a strong and supportive education and training system to support its workers in the new world of work.

3.3. Labour market information system (LMIS) as a tool to provide better estimates of skills needs

3.3.1. Public professional training needs to be responsive to changes in the labour market and skill needs

Professional training provided by the State, prefectures and the private sector – called 'vocational' training in Japan – aims to help participants' reskill and upskill in view of finding employment or develop their career, particularly in in-demand and growing sectors. To achieve this goal, it is important to ensure that training is responsive to changes in the labour market and skill needs.

Re-employment figures for participants in public vocational training in Japan have been quite high. The employment rate three months after completion of training provided by either the State or prefectures was 84% for unemployed individuals in FY2020, and 71% in FY2020 for training outsourced to the private sector (Ministry of Health, Labour and Welfare, 2022[10]). More rigorous evaluations confirm this finding. Research into the employment effects of training using the propensity score matching methods has confirmed that attending public vocational training increases the likelihood of employment, regardless of the type of training (Ministry of Health, Labour and Welfare, 2022[11]) This is in line with international evidence from cross-country meta-analyses also showing that training is, on average, effective in promoting employment one or more years after programme completion, although there is wide variation in the country-level estimates (Card, Kluve and Weber, 2017[12])

However, there is still room to improve public vocational training to make it more responsive to changes in skill needs due to megatrends such as digitalisation, globalisation and unexpected shocks such as the COVID-19 pandemic. Although the provision of public vocational training for the unemployed has evolved in line with the changing demand for training and other factors (as discussed below), a rough mapping of trainees and labour market openings by occupation shows that there is not proportional strong relationship between the number of people attending job-related training or the volume of job offers within that occupation (Panel A and B of Figure 3.7). The relationship with shortages is also weak and negative, when using the OECD Skills for Jobs Indicators which measure shortages (demand exceeds supply) and surplus (supply exceeds demand) across occupations in over 40 countries, including Japan (Panel C of Figure 3.7) For instance, in Japan, a significant number of participants attend training for service and clerical jobs (business administration) while these occupations are in surplus. Comparatively, long-term care faces a relatively high shortage in workers but a low number of training participants.

Figure 3.7. The number of participants in public vocational training does not necessarily correspond to the demand for jobs as a whole

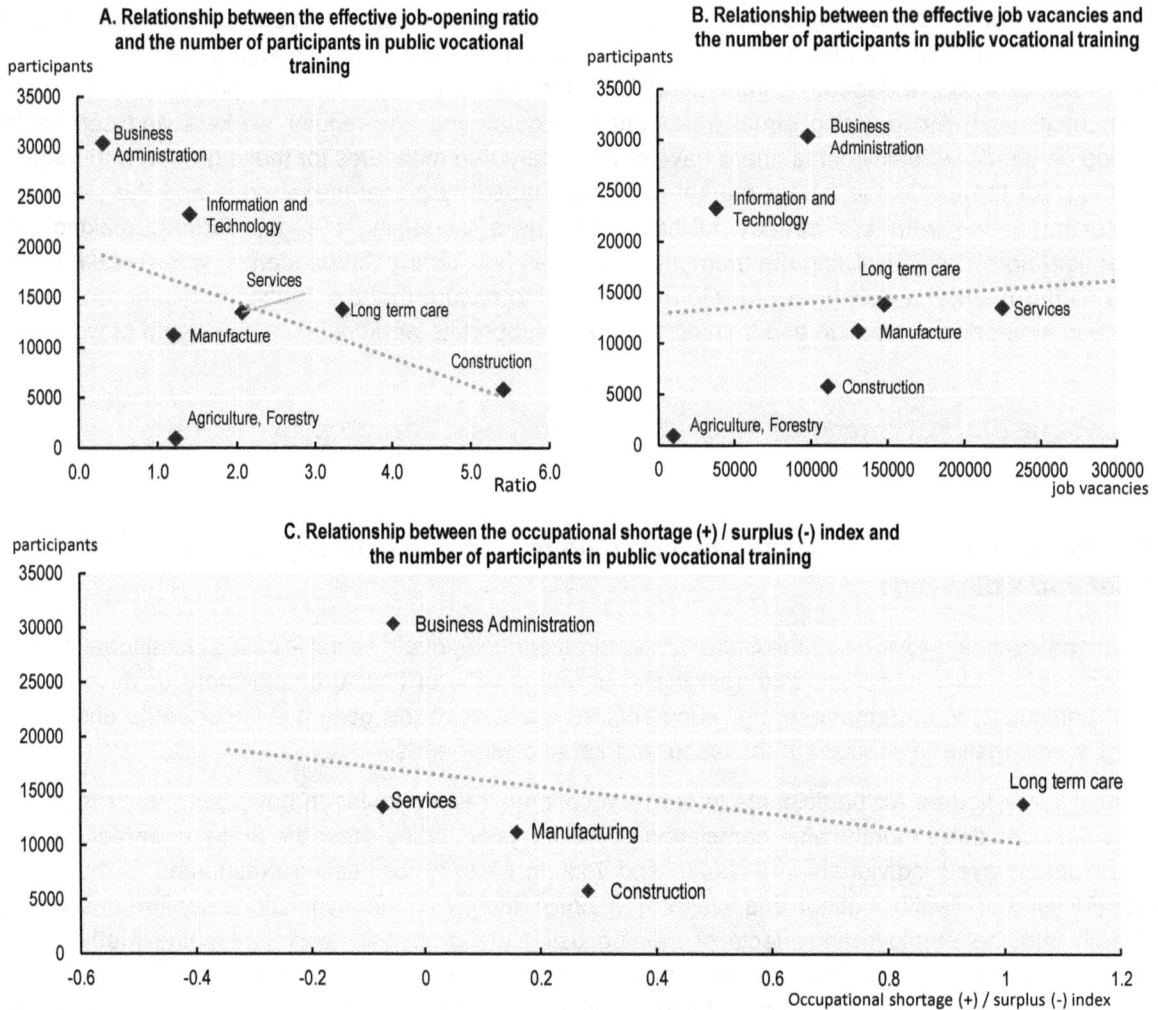

A. Relationship between the effective job-opening ratio and the number of participants in public vocational training

participants

- Business Administration
- Information and Technology
- Services
- Long term care
- Manufacture
- Construction
- Agriculture, Forestry

Ratio

B. Relationship between the effective job vacancies and the number of participants in public vocational training

participants

- Business Administration
- Information and Technology
- Long term care
- Services
- Manufacture
- Construction
- Agriculture, Forestry

job vacancies

C. Relationship between the occupational shortage (+) / surplus (-) index and the number of participants in public vocational training

participants

- Business Administration
- Services
- Manufacturing
- Construction
- Long term care

Occupational shortage (+) / surplus (-) index

Note: The effective job-opening ratio is defined as the ratio between the number of job openings and the number of job seekers registered at Hello Work. The effective job-opening ratio and the number of effective job vacancies are averages for FY 2020. The number of participants in public vocational training is for FY 2020. Occupational shortage (+) / surplus (-) index is for 2018. The occupation of the effective job-opening ratio and the effective job vacancies are classified based on occupational classification in the public employment service. The occupation of occupational shortage (+) / surplus (-) index are classified based on the Labour Force Survey.

Source: OECD calculations based on report on Employment Service by the Ministry of Health, Labour and Welfare, MHLW (2022[10]), Hello Training (public vocational training) (Actual results for fiscal years 2017 to 2021), https://www.mhlw.go.jp/content/11801000/000894633.pdf; and OECD Skills for Jobs Database, www.oecdskillsforjobsdatabase.org.

It should be noted that public vocational training is generally provided for sectors where little private provision is available. Irrespective, there is scope to make public vocational training more responsive to changing skill needs.

3.3.2. Better labour market information systems can help policy makers plan adult learning and career guidance strategically

Building better labour marker information system can help understand changes in the labour market and skills needs in real time, so that policy makers can quickly adapt their training provision and career guidance services.

The decision-making process for public vocational training in Japan

Public vocational training in Japan is provided in accordance with the Plan for the Implementation of Vocational Training prepared by the Minister of Health, Labour and Welfare, based on the Law for the Promotion of Vocational Skills Development. The plan is decided by the Central Training Council, which includes representatives from labour, management, academics, education-related organisations and relevant ministries and agencies. It is elaborated based on discussions of the focus areas of skills development policies and considering the determinants of future skill needs trend at national level, such as sectors suffering from shortages or growing sectors. Thereafter, at the regional level, each of the 47 prefectures in Japan formulates its own plan after discussions with the Prefectural Training Councils, in which local business sectors, training providers, and local labour bureaus participate. The prefectures decide on target areas and on the scale of training programme implementation to address local skill needs, based on the direction discussed at the Central Training Council. These national and prefectural plans are updated every year.

Previously, prefectural councils were not backed by law and there were no explicit rules for the operation of the councils in each prefecture. In response, the Government of Japan amended the Law for the Promotion of Vocational Skills Development in 2022 to facilitate the establishment of more appropriate public vocational training courses are the regional level. This amendment makes it a statutory requirement to establish a consultative forum comprised of a wide range of stakeholders, including: local labour and management organisations; education and training institutions including universities; labour bureaus; prefectures; and job placement agencies (Ministry of Health, Labour and Welfare, 2022[13]). The councils can conduct hearings of individual cases, for example, from companies that have employed participants of public vocational training or from the training participants themselves, to ascertain training needs and the training effects of individual courses. The prefectural councils can also be used to discuss how to develop career counselling services and employment support.

Central training councils and local councils are powerful tools that can co-ordinate with various ministries and stakeholders who hold data on training, labour market, and education. At the moment, however, information systems are not fully utilised to analyse current skill needs and assess future trends when planning training provision. The Training Council mainly discusses the type and scale of training to be provided in the following year, based on existing government policy and data on applications for public vocational training in the most recent year, the number of training participants in the previous years and their employment rate. The training plan is also constrained by the fact that the total amount of training is subject to government budgetary constraints, and the number of trainings cannot be significantly changed in the absence of enough budget. The scale of public vocational training therefore depends more on the most recent training participation results, rather than mismatch or future estimates based on the demand for skills such as specific qualifications (technical, vocational, university, etc.), fields (law, medicine, economics, etc.) or specific skills (numeracy, literacy, problem solving, soft skills, etc.). Indeed, the documents used for discussion at the Central Training Council do not include quantitative data relating to skills (Ministry of Health, Labour and Welfare, 2022[14]).

Figure 3.8. Data on skills are not often used in discussions on the size and content of public vocational training

The National Training Council's membership and the information examined in making planning decisions

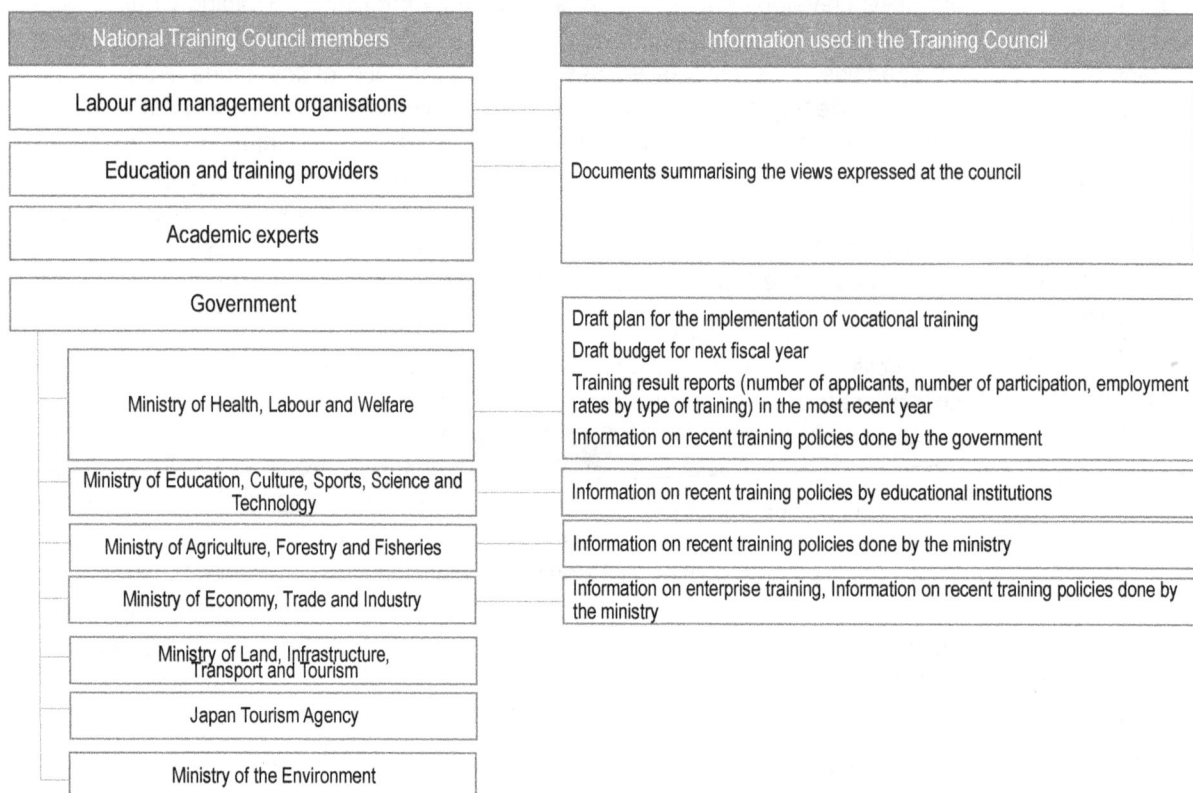

National Training Council members	Information used in the Training Council
Labour and management organisations	Documents summarising the views expressed at the council
Education and training providers	
Academic experts	
Government	
Ministry of Health, Labour and Welfare	Draft plan for the implementation of vocational training Draft budget for next fiscal year Training result reports (number of applicants, number of participation, employment rates by type of training) in the most recent year Information on recent training policies done by the government
Ministry of Education, Culture, Sports, Science and Technology	Information on recent training policies by educational institutions
Ministry of Agriculture, Forestry and Fisheries	Information on recent training policies done by the ministry
Ministry of Economy, Trade and Industry	Information on enterprise training, Information on recent training policies done by the ministry
Ministry of Land, Infrastructure, Transport and Tourism	
Japan Tourism Agency	
Ministry of the Environment	

Source: Prepared by authors based on materials from the 2022 National Training Council, available at: https://www.mhlw.go.jp/stf/shingi/other-syokunou_128998.html.

Not using quantitative demand forecasts focusing on skills and tasks when setting up training plan may be related to traditional employment practices in Japan. Japanese employment practices have been characterised by lifetime employment, a seniority-based wage system and the regular intake of new graduates (OECD, 2021[2]). In this context, adult learning has been primarily provided by firms through on-the-job training, where training has been based on career change within the same company according to the company's needs, rather than skill-specific training.

However, in recent years, this situation has changed. In 2018, the government issued guidelines targeting labour market flexibility and creating conditions that would support job changes at all ages, and in order to better match workers who want to change jobs with companies, an amendment was made in 2020 to impose an obligation on large companies to publish the percentage of mid-career hires (OECD, 2021[15]). In addition, the new Japanese O*NET database (called "job tag") was released in 2020, and has made it possible to visualise the skills required for each occupation, gradually making skill-focused research possible. "Job tag" provides a comprehensive overview of a wide range of labour market information for around 500 occupations, including job descriptions, required education and qualifications, degree of vocational training required before and after employment, number of workers, working hours, average wages, average age and other working conditions, labour shortage conditions, required skills, knowledge and work values. The number of "job tag" page views exceeded 2 million in FY2020 when it was launched and 5 million in FY2021. The platform is steadily attracting a large number of users. The information accumulated could be incorporated into the labour market information system (LMIS) to enable even more effective policy decision-making.

Developing a better Labour Market Information system (LMIS)

A LMIS is "a network of institutions, persons and information that have mutually recognised roles, agreements and functions with respect to the production, storage, dissemination and use of labour market related information and results in order to maximise the potential for relevant and applicable policy and programme formulation and implementation" (ILO, n.d.[16]). Ideally, an LMIS provides a foundation for employment and labour policies, informing the design, implementation, monitoring and evaluation of more focused policies.

In general, labour market information includes the following information and intelligence (Hofer, Zhivkovikj and Smyth, 2020[17]):

1. Labour market conditions (national and/or regional), including demand and supply trends
2. Projections of future demand and supply
3. Occupational trends and opportunities
4. Skills requirements and links between training and education and careers
5. Interpretation and analysis of data (Woods and O'Leary, 2006[18])

An LMIS helps labour market actors overcome incomplete information and thus contributes to reducing labour market transaction costs. Providing information on market needs such as skills, tasks and other market needs for specific occupations in an LMIS not only assists government data-driven decision-making with regard to training policy, but also helps jobseekers find vocational training to develop the right skills or to be matched effectively in job placement (UNESCO, 2018[19]).

A labour market information system consists of four main elements: 1) collection and compilation of data and information; 2) information storage; 3) analytical capacities and tools; and 4) institutional arrangements and networks (ILO, n.d.[16]). In Japan, labour-related data such as the Labour Force Survey and the Basic Survey on Wage Structure have been collected and stored through government statistics portals (e-stat), and these data have been used for policy making through regular analysis or forecasting future demand and supply. At present, however, interpretation and analysis on skills and vocational training is limited, with the exception of the Basic Survey of Human Resource Development, which is an official statistic, and other databases such as "job tag", which have been launched in recent years. Institutional arrangements for analysing and utilising such information in the training policy making process are still developing. In other countries such as Canada, LMISs are strategically constructed and skills-related data is analysed by experts including labour economists and statisticians (Box 3.1).

On the one hand, as mentioned above, the collection and construction of skills databases has gradually progressed in Japan, following the launch of the "job tag" and other developments. On the other hand, the analytical and institutional capacity to make the most of the data collected is still insufficient. Understanding the relationships between occupations in terms of skill composition is a new approach in Japan. For instance, it requires mapping skill sets by occupational category and generating skill similarity scores between occupations. These similarity scores enable the investigation of potential job changes based on current and past occupations and areas for further skills development of individuals to facilitate alternative career paths (Mustafa Sayedi, Aryeh Ansel, 2021[20]). These skills matching and gap analyses provide new insights for potential career changes and also help policy makers to determine effective training programmes. However, these are still new approaches and require refinement and deepening and they also require changes to the skill system to adapt it to make use of the data.

Box 3.1. Labour Market Information System in Canada and Singapore

Labour Market Information Council in Canada

In 2017, the Labour Market Information Council (LMIC) was established with the aim of enabling Canadians to make evidence-based decisions by providing access to high-quality, relevant and comprehensive skills-related data and its analysis across the LMI ecosystem across Canada. LMIC is a pan-Canadian not-for-profit organisation and governed by a Board of Directors and three subcommittees including Executive, Audit and Strategy and Evaluation. The LMIC Board of Directors is comprised of 15 representatives from each province and territory as well as states (Employment and Social Development Canada and Statistics Canada). It is responsible for setting the direction and priorities of LMIC in consultation with stakeholders. LMIC Staff consists of labour and digital specialists such as economists, data scientists, and engineers.

The Career Guidance Stakeholder Committee was recently established to ensure that the particular needs of career guidance delivery system and its clients are accommodated. The committee is responsible to ensure that all activities such as producing new skills and related labour market information and deciding channels of delivery are evidence-based and impactful.

Recognising that vast amounts of labour market information are often dispersed across multiple sources and only available for specialists, LMIC, in collaboration with the Future Skills Centre (FSC), has launched a high quality LMI data cloud-based repository. The LMIC Data Hub is a Google Cloud Platform-based database in which information is stored and made easily accessible to people.

SkillsFuture in Singapore

The SkillsFuture aims to encourage the development of autonomous leaners by providing ongoing education and training opportunities to help them stay current with the ever-changing marketplace. A key feature of the website is to act as a gateway for the provision of SkillsFuture credits to all resident aged 25 and above that can be used to pay for pre-approved learning and skills development courses.

SkillsFuture is a statutory body operating under the Ministry of Education, which work closely with other government organisation (Workforce Singapore) to create a nation of agile workers and embrace the spirit of lifelong learning. It plans to expand the course list continually in consultation with employers and industry partners. A Training Management System provides APIs (Application Programming Interface) to retrieve information on sector, career pathways, occupations and job roles, related training and skills.

Source: LMIC (https://lmic-cimt.ca/); OECD (2022[21]), *Career Guidance for Adults in Canada*, https://doi.org/10.1787/0e596882-en; Barnes and Bimrose (2021[22]), "Labour market information and its use to inform career guidance of young people" https://warwick.ac.uk/fac/soc/ier/research/lmicareerguidanceofyoungpeople/ier_gatsby_lmis_landscape_2021_final.pdf; SkillsFuture (https://www.skillsfuture.gov.sg).

Effective use of labour market information through online portals across Japan

Once information is collected in an efficient LMIS, it is important that it feeds into policy actions to enable jobseekers, companies and career consultants to obtain timely, up-to-date and representative labour and training information. Quality information allows jobseekers to search for jobs, receive effective career guidance and participate in training that is aligned with labour market needs. Various portals to access information on education and vocational training are now available in Japan, including: the website encouraging adult learning (*Manapass*); the website set up by the Ministry of Health, Labour and Welfare's listing courses eligible for training benefits; the public employment service's website for jobseekers; the Job Card website for career development; and an occupational information website. Although each website has a different purpose, the lack of co-ordination translates into scattered information across different government portals (OECD, 2021[15]).

In this regards, it is noteworthy that the government now plans to strengthen the link between the Public Employment Service's online job-seeking information and "job tag" (Cabinet Secretariat, 2022[23]). Bringing information on "job tag" and job search information together will help jobseekers make better decisions by enabling them to effectively identify the skills in high demand. Linking these information with vocational training currently offered could further lead to use of public employment services and directing people to public vocational training.

For instance, South Korea provides a centralised system that includes comprehensive information on the skills required of workers, job matching, relevant vocational training, and educational institutions, through collaborative partnerships with the private sector and the use of advanced technology solutions including artificial intelligence (AI) (Box 3.2).

Box 3.2. A comprehensive labour and training information platform (Work-net) in Korea

Work-net is operated by the Korea Employment Information Service (KEIS) under the Ministry of Employment and Labour (MoEL) and provides job matching and a comprehensive labour and training information. Work-net provides functions other than job matching either directly or in conjunction with the Korean LMIS sub-system.

For example, it is linked to the Korea Network for Occupations and Workers for career and skills guidance and to HRD-net for vocational training. HRD-net offers vocational training courses and qualification tests, and key statistics on vocational training, which are provided in conjunction with job vacancies on Work-net. This information includes training course content, training objectives, application requirements, relevant qualifications, training duration, training costs, government subsidies, training personnel, training facilities and post-training employment outcomes. People can search Work-net's vocational training information and apply for support for training on their computers or smartphones; Work-net and HRD-net systems and data are linked and interoperable. It also provides information on employment and welfare policies at national and local government level and links to other ministries and public authorities.

KEIS uses the information in the LMIS for evaluation, analysis, and forecasting, with the objective of helping to design, monitor, and evaluate public policy at the national, regional, and local levels. Work-net also shares information through an API (Application Programming Interface). Its functioning is supported by strong institutional arrangements involving the private sector, central and local government, the education system, a strong technical infrastructure for information sharing and advanced technological solutions (big data, artificial intelligence) to efficiently analyse data and disseminate available information.

Work-net consists of national and public job information providers, private operators, regional governments, and public vocational centres under MoEL. It has partnered with over 170 organisations to establish institutional arrangements for access to job vacancies. Private providers are free to post jobs on Work-net in addition to public employment services, but due to a multi-layered verification system involving artificial intelligence and multiple experts, only 60% of all jobs are posted, and the legal quality jobs that meet the requirements are guaranteed by the government.

Work-net also has a dedicated marketing team to attract job seekers, and works on proactive marketing activities and events, targeting specific groups (e.g. youth), promoting partnerships (e.g. universities) and disseminating research results to potential users. It has won various customer satisfaction and brand-related awards (App Award Korea, Good Brand Trusted by Consumers, Korea Top Public Service Award, Top 10 Public Apps Loved by the People, Korea National Service Satisfaction Award). In 2018, the number of registered users reached approximately 16 million.

Source: WORKNET (https://www.work.go.kr/seekWantedMain.do); World Bank Group (2021[24]), https://openknowledge.worldbank.org/bitstream/handle/10986/35378/Toward-a-World-Class-Labor-Market-Information-System-for-Indonesia-An-Assessment-of-the-System-Managed-by.pdf?sequence=1&isAllowed=y.

A virtuous circle to promote training of workers

A high-quality LMIS could lead to improved quality of career guidance provided by firms and career consultants, as well as further training support for workers in companies. Workers' training opportunities are then expected to increase thanks to the support provided by firms and career consultants. Indeed, the probability of participation in off-the-job training is correlated with career guidance experiences and company support. An econometric analysis shows that the probability of undertaking off-the-job training is 6 percentage points higher for workers in companies that have put in place mechanisms for career guidance, compared with workers in other companies. In addition, workers who experienced career guidance in the past year are 17 percentage points more likely to undertake off-the-job training in the same year than workers who have not, although it should be noted that some selection bias may exist (Figure 3.9).

This situation is also the same for workers' self-development. Workers who work a company that provide career consulting support are 5 percentage points more likely to undertake off-the-job training than workers in other company. Workers in companies that provide financial support such as course fees for self-development are 3 percentage points more likely to undertake self-development, and 5 percentage points more likely to undertake self-development if their company provides information such as education and training institutions and online learning. The adult learning market in Japan can be further expanded by creating a virtuous circle of worker participation in training by linking a good labour market information system with the provision of appropriate vocational training and career guidance.

Figure 3.9. Effects of off-the-job training and self-development implementation by worker's characteristics and firm's support

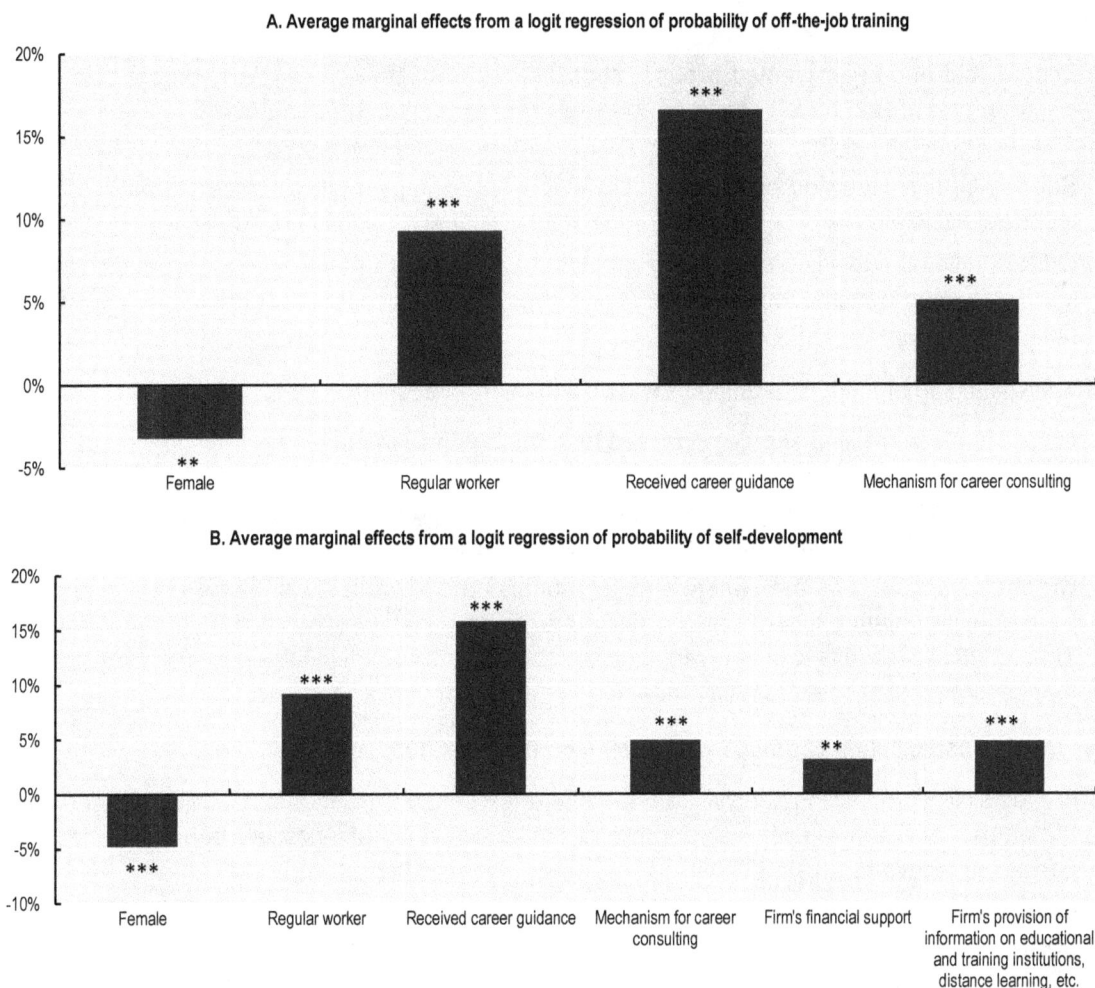

A. Average marginal effects from a logit regression of probability of off-the-job training

B. Average marginal effects from a logit regression of probability of self-development

Note: ***, statistically significant at the 1% level, **, statistically significant at the 5% level and *, statistically significant at the 10% level. The figure shows estimates of the average marginal impact of selected variables on receiving off-the-job training and undertaking worker's self-development. The benchmark group is male and non-regular worker. "Received career guidance" is a dummy variable for whether or not the respondent has participated on career guidance in the last year. "Mechanism for career consulting" is a dummy variable for whether or not the firm has some kind of career counselling mechanism, whether institutionalised or not. "Firms' financial support" is a dummy variable for whether or not firms provide workers with financial assistance, such as course fees, for worker's self-development. These effects are estimated with controls for age, years of experience, industry, occupation, job title, working hours, firm sizes, turnover rate, percentage of non-regular workers in a firm, and others.
Source: OECD analysis based on Japanese Basic Survey of Human Resource Development (2020) supported by the Ministry of Health, Labour and Welfare.

Policy recommendations

Expand the use of online training

- Ensure that underrepresented groups, such as older adults, non-regular workers and those living in rural areas, have access to courses on basic digital skills in-person to prevent them from falling behind in the digitalisation of public services and training.
- Support both private and public providers who want to implement distance learning, through technical assistance and certification of full online training for public providers.
- Offer additional subsidies for training providers who want to trial delivery of real-time online learning and on-demand recorded training courses, while taking into account outcomes such as post-training employment rates.

Support the scaling up of modular training provision and micro-credentials

- Introduce skills profiling and personalised learning pathways to tailor the training plan of adults to their skills and experience. Individualised training programmes that factor in both local labour market demand and the adult's past experience have a higher chance of leading to sustainable employment, and should be used in public training facilities.
- Create training programmes where smaller modules are rewarded with partial credits, and can be stacked to attain a fully-credited training programme that is recognised by the government. This would allow adults to circumvent time constraints and complete larger training programmes that have previously been unattainable due to the length of the courses.

Increase training participation of groups with lower labour market outcomes

- Exploit skills composition analysis to understand the best upskilling and reskilling opportunities for women and non-regular workers in order to ensure they are not 'left behind' in the post-pandemic recovery.
- Leverage career guidance and upskilling opportunities to increase the hiring of women in positions where they are underrepresented, such as occupations with high leadership skills and high technical skills.

Leverage existing data to create analytical tools to assess and anticipate skills needs

- Perform an extensive mapping of existing labour information data and sources, including governmental data, local data and information originating in research centres. Create an overview of the data synergy and key indicators that can be tracked to analyse skills supply and demand.
- Create a real-time labour market information system (LMIS) that runs automatically and is updated on a regular basis, as well as forward-looking labour market projections. Evaluate which public institution or department is best equipped to manage the programme and co-ordinate the stakeholders who provide data input.
- Create a structured and extensive dissemination plan for the LMIS. On a granular level, the tool should be shared with key stakeholders and practitioners involved in training and career guidance. The government should actively draw upon the analysis in the LMIS when creating and evaluating skill and labour-related policies, such as policies on training, career guidance, industry restructuring and investment.

References

Barnes, S. and J. Bimrose (2021), "Labour market information and its use to inform career guidance of young people", https://warwick.ac.uk/fac/soc/ier/research/lmicareerguidanceofyoungpeople/ier_gatsby_lmis_l andscape_2021_final.pdf. [22]

Cabinet Secretariat (2022), "Follow-up on the grand design and implementation plan of the new capitalism", https://www.cas.go.jp/jp/seisaku/atarashii_sihonsyugi/pdf/fu2022.pdf. [23]

Card, D., J. Kluve and A. Weber (2017), "What Works? A Meta Analysis of Recent Active Labor Market Program Evaluations", *Journal of the European Economic Association*, Vol. 16/3, pp. 894-931, https://doi.org/10.1093/jeea/jvx028. [12]

European Commission/EACEA/Eurydice (2021), *Adult education and training in Europe: Building inclusive pathways to skills and qualifications*, Publications Office of the European Union, https://doi.org/10.2797/898965. [8]

Eurostat (2021), *Labour Force Survey*, https://ec.europa.eu/eurostat/web/lfs/data/database (accessed on 1 July 2022). [4]

Fouarge, D., T. Schils and A. de Grip (2012), "Why do low-educated workers invest less in further training?", *Applied Economics*, Vol. 45/18, pp. 2587-2601, https://doi.org/10.1080/00036846.2012.671926. [7]

Hofer, A., A. Zhivkovikj and R. Smyth (2020), "The role of labour market information in guiding educational and occupational choices", *OECD Education Working Papers*, No. 229, OECD Publishing, Paris, https://doi.org/10.1787/59bbac06-en. [17]

ILO (n.d.), "Labour Market Information Systems (LMIS)", https://ilostat.ilo.org/resources/labour-market-information-systems/#:~:text=A%20labour%20market%20information%20system,the%20potential%20for%20relevant%20and. [16]

Ministry of Economy, Trade and Industry (2020), "Report of the Study Group on Improvement of Sustainable Corporate Value and Human Capital", https://www.meti.go.jp/shingikai/economy/kigyo_kachi_kojo/pdf/20200930_1e.pdf (accessed on 2 June 2022). [3]

Ministry of Health, Labour and Welfare (2022), "Central Training Council", https://www.mhlw.go.jp/stf/shingi/other-syokunou_128998.html. [14]

Ministry of Health, Labour and Welfare (2022), "Effectiveness analysis of public vocational training", https://www.mhlw.go.jp/content/12602000/000943952.pdf. [11]

Ministry of Health, Labour and Welfare (2022), "Hello Training (public vocational training) (Actual results for fiscal years 2017 to 2021)", https://www.mhlw.go.jp/content/11801000/000894633.pdf. [10]

Ministry of Health, Labour and Welfare (2022), "Legislation submitted to the 208th session of the Diet (2022 Standing Session)", https://www.mhlw.go.jp/stf/topics/bukyoku/soumu/houritu/208.html. [13]

Ministry of Health, Labour and Welfare (2018), "Outline of the "Act on the Arrangement of Related Acts to Promote Work Style Reform" (Act No. 71 of 2018)", https://www.mhlw.go.jp/english/policy/employ-labour/labour-standards/dl/201904kizyun.pdf (accessed on 2 June 2022). [1]

Ministry of Internal Affairs and Communications (2016), "Administrative evaluation and monitoring of the effective implementation of vocational development with a focus on vocational training", https://www.soumu.go.jp/main_content/000396885.pdf. [5]

Mustafa Sayedi, Aryeh Ansel (2021), "Labour Market Information in Responsive Career Pathways", https://fsc-ccf.ca/wp-content/uploads/2021/11/FSC-RCP-LMI-EN.pdf. [20]

OECD (2022), *Career Guidance for Adults in Canada*, Getting Skills Right, OECD Publishing, Paris, https://doi.org/10.1787/0e596882-en. [21]

OECD (2022), *OECD Employment Outlook 2022: Building Back More Inclusive Labour Markets*, OECD Publishing, Paris, https://doi.org/10.1787/1bb305a6-en. [9]

OECD (2021), *Creating Responsive Adult Learning Opportunities in Japan*, Getting Skills Right, OECD Publishing, Paris, https://doi.org/10.1787/cfe1ccd2-en. [2]

OECD (2021), *OECD Economic Surveys: Japan 2021*, OECD Publishing, Paris, https://doi.org/10.1787/6b749602-en. [15]

OECD (2020), "The potential of online learning for adults: Early lessons from the COVID-19 crisis", *OECD Policy Responses to Coronavirus (COVID-19)*, OECD Publishing, Paris, https://doi.org/10.1787/ee040002-en. [6]

UNESCO (2018), *Review on Labor Market Information System (LMIS) in Lebanon*. [19]

Woods, J. and C. O'Leary (2006), *Conceptual Framework for an Optimal Labour Market Information System: Final Report*, W.E. Upjohn Institute, https://doi.org/10.17848/tr07-022. [18]

World Bank Group (2021), "Toward a World-Class Labor Market Information System for Indonesia", https://openknowledge.worldbank.org/bitstream/handle/10986/35378/Toward-a-World-Class-Labor-Market-Information-System-for-Indonesia-An-Assessment-of-the-System-Managed-by.pdf?sequence=1&isAllowed=y. [24]

www.ingramcontent.com/pod-product-compliance
Lightning Source LLC
Chambersburg PA
CBHW082109210326
41599CB00033B/6645